GCSE
ENGLISH for CCEA

Noreen Doran
Ellen McVea
Kate O'Hanlon
Len Quigg
Pauline Wylie

media

writer's craft

non-fiction

analyse

fiction

media

purpose

evaluate

Hodder Murray

A MEMBER OF THE HODDER HEADLINE GROUP

cea

Rewarding Learning

Acknowledgements

The author and publishers would like to thank the following for:

Copyright text:
p. 11 © *Carrie's War* by Nina Bawden, Puffin Books; pp. 15–16 © *In Love with an Urban Gorilla: Recycled Confessions* by Steve Skidmore and Steve Barlow. Reproduced with permission of Piccadilly Press; pp. 18–19 'Neilly and The Fir Tree' from *Irish Short Stories* by John O'Connor, ed. Frances Crowe, Literary Executor John Boyd for story from *Threshold*, no. 21, summer 1967, published by the Lyric Players Theatre; pp. 24–25 Extract from *Badger on the Barge* by Janni Howker © 1984 Janni Howker. Reproduced by permission of Walker Books, London, SE11 5HJ; pp. 42–43 © 'Statements of Account' by Jenny Hursell from *Knockout: Short Stories*, Longman 1988; pp. 44–45 © 'Uneasy Homecoming' by Will Jenkins from *The Quickening Pulse 2*, Hodder & Stoughton; pp. 48–50 'Aristocrockery' from *One Grand Sweet Song* by Sam McBratney, Mammoth Irish 1999; pp. 52–55 © 'The Trap' from *Oranges from Spain and Other Stories* by David Park. Reproduced by permission of The Sayle Literary Agency; pp. 81–82 'Postcard from Canberra' © Jeremy Atiyah, *The Independent on Sunday*, Traveller Supplement, 21 September 2003; pp. 83–84 'Beyond the Hutch' © Justine Hankins, *The Guardian*, Weekend, 28 September 2002; p. 97 Reproduced by kind permission of the Cyprus Tourist Office; p. 99 'The New Look That Could Scar You For Life' © Victoria Fletcher, *Sunday Express*, 26 August 2001; p. 102 'Child's Play' © Rosie Waterhouse, *The Sunday Times*, 14 May 2000; pp. 103–104 © Exploris, Northern Ireland Aquarium; pp. 107–109 © Northern Ireland Child Protection Committee; p. 110 'Why I can't wait for it all to be over for England' © Peter Hitchens, *The Mail on Sunday*, 2 June 2002; pp. 112–114 © *The Road to McCarthy*, Pete McCarthy, Hodder Headline; pp. 130–131 'Can't Jog, Won't Jog' © Candida Crewe, *The Times Magazine*, 19 October 2002.

Copyright photographs:
p. 3 © Michael St. Maur Sheil/CORBIS; p. 30 © Popperfoto; p. 33 & 35 © Bettmann/CORBIS; p. 57 © Marvyl/CORBIS; p. 66 © Arthur Jumper/Life File Photo Library; p. 79 © Michael Boys/CORBIS; p. 82 © Paul A. Souders/CORBIS; p. 91 © Ron Watts/CORBIS; p.93 © Flip Schulke/CORBIS; p. 110 © actionplus sports images; p. 117 © Belfast City Airport; p. 124 *top* © Phillipa Lewis; Edifice/CORBIS, *bottom* © Eric Crichton/CORBIS; p. 125 *top* © Spike Powell; Elizabeth Whiting & Associates/CORBIS, *bottom* © Clay Perry/CORBIS.

Copyright artwork:
All artwork © Corinne and Ray Burrows (Beehive Illustration).

Every effort has been made to trace copyright holders of material reproduced in this book. Any rights not acknowledged here will be acknowledged in subsequent printings if notice is given to the publisher.

Orders: please contact Bookpoint Ltd, 130 Milton Park, Abingdon, Oxon OX14 4SB. Telephone: (44)01235 827720. Fax: (44)01235 400454. Lines are open from 9.00–5.00, Monday to Saturday, with a 24-hour message answering service. You can also order through our website www.hodderheadline.co.uk.

British Library Cataloguing in Publication Data
A catalogue record for this title is available from the British Library.

ISBN: 978 0 340 85727 4

First Published 2003

Impression number   10 9 8 7 6
Year   2009 2008 2007

Copyright © 2003 John Andrews, Noreen Doran, Ellen McVea, Kate O'Hanlon, Len Quigg, Pauline Wylie

Typeset by Fakenham Photosetting Limited, Fakenham, Norfolk
Printed in Italy for Hodder Murray, a division of Hodder Education, an Hachette Livre UK company, 338 Euston Road, London NW1 3BH.

CONTENTS

PAPER 2

SECTION A Writing to inform, explain and describe

SECTION B Reading: Response to non-fiction and media texts

INTRODUCTION

The make-up of CCEA's GCSE English course

CCEA's GCSE English examination is made up of two written exams worth 60% of the overall mark and a coursework element that is worth the remaining 40%. The coursework consists of:

a   Talking and listening   20%
b   Reading and writing   20%.

The coursework section of the GCSE course is not dealt with in this text, but it is obvious that if you are to maximise your overall performance then you will have to ensure that you do as well as you can in these important elements of the exam.

The purpose of this text

Its aim is simple – to help you deal as successfully as you can with the end-of-course examination.

The GCSE English examination is not designed to try to catch you out nor is it designed to spring nasty surprises upon you. It is built around the idea that you, as a candidate, should be given a fair opportunity to show your ability in the subject – what you can do, rather than what you can't.

In order to help you succeed it is essential that you understand the demands and skills required by each of the four sections within the two exams:

Paper 1   Section A: Testing **reading** through an unseen literary prose text

Section B: Testing **writing** skills: to review, analyse and comment

Paper 2   Section A: Testing **writing** skills: to inform, explain and describe

Section B: Testing **reading** through non-fiction and media texts.

Each of these four sections is designed to meet the requirements of a range of assessment objectives (a collective term for the specific skills and abilities in which you are being tested). These will be explained as each new section is analysed.

This book focuses on each of these assessment areas in turn, helping you by describing and analysing the individual skills that make up each element. After these have been practised individually, they are then reassembled before you are asked to take on a complete GCSE task.

Each section of the book finishes off with sample papers that accurately mirror the demands made at both foundation and higher tier.

We hope you will find that, as a result of working your way through this text, you have a clearer understanding of what you have to do and how to go about answering your GCSE English papers in an appropriate manner.

PAPER 1
SECTION A
Reading: Response to a literary prose text

THE ASSESSMENT OBJECTIVES

These are the skills and abilities that this **reading** section tests.

The percentage of the marks given to the different assessment objectives

100%

Students are expected to show the ability to:

a   read with insight and engagement

b   develop an interpretation of a text

c   select suitable points from a text

d   understand and assess how writers use language and structure to bring about their desired effects.

1 What's required?

By the time you have worked through this section you should be equipped to tackle what is one of the most challenging sections of the whole exam. You will have **one hour** in which to read about **120 lines of a literary prose text** you will not have seen before and then answer **three questions** on it.

You will be expected to demonstrate the ability to analyse:

a character
b relationships between characters
c setting
d the writer's craft.

The first two of these questions will require you to show your understanding of **what** the writer has done, focusing on character, situation and setting; in the final question you will be required to look at **how** the author has developed the piece of writing – the writer's craft.

---

2 Understanding character

What's required?

You will be expected to show an understanding of how character is created in fiction. In order to do this you will have to come to conclusions about characters. Below you will be shown how this is done.

The methods through which we understand characters in fiction are similar to how we find out what people are like in real life. Our knowledge of other people comes from:

▸ their appearance
▸ what they say
▸ what they do
▸ what they think
▸ what other people say about them
▸ how other people react to them.

When reading fiction you need to be aware of all of these things and what they suggest about the character. You also need to remember that all of the information is coming directly to you from one person, the author. Remember that the author might want to guide or influence your response to the character.

The character's appearance

In real life it is unwise to judge someone based on their appearance, but when you are reading fiction you should be aware of how a character's physical appearance is described. This can help you make up your mind about the author's opinion of the character and how the writer wants you to feel about that person.

ACTIVITY 1

Read the following passage in which a young boy called Pip visits an old lady called Miss Havisham. Work out what sort of a person Miss Havisham is by talking through the points that follow the passage.

In an armchair, with an elbow resting on the table and her head leaning on that hand, sat the strangest lady I have ever seen, or ever shall see.

She was dressed in rich materials – satins, and lace, and silks – all of white. Her shoes were white. And she had a long white veil dependent from her hair, and she had bridal flowers in her hair; but her hair was white . . . She had not quite finished dressing, for she had but one shoe on – the other was on the table near her hand – her veil was but half arranged, her watch and chain were not put on.

From *Great Expectations* by Charles Dickens

There are many clues in this short passage about Miss Havisham.

▸ She is sitting in an armchair with her head resting on her hand – could this be because she is tired or unhappy? Can you suggest any other possible reason?
▸ She is dressed in 'rich materials' – could this suggest she is a wealthy woman, or is she dressed for a special occasion?
▸ She is wearing white clothes and white shoes – is there any significance in the colour?
▸ She has 'not quite finished dressing' – what clues are there in the passage that she has been interrupted while dressing?

What do you think might have happened?

ACTIVITY 2

Below is another passage in which a character's physical appearance is described. Read it and answer the questions that follow.

He came in, making the room small. The skin on his face was mottled with the shock of cold water. His eyelids were rimmed with red as though his eyes had been always shut and forgotten but had now suddenly been slit open with a sharp blade to reveal surprised and bulging brown eyes, the whites all yellowed with waiting. His lashes, too, seemed as though they had this minute been put there, standing stiff and straight like glued bristles.

Mostly, Uncle's face was long and thin, with big folds of skin hanging down, but his cheekbones were round and jutting. His nose was hooked at the tip, with a big bubble of flesh at either side.

He wore the top half of a football jersey. . .and he carried a billy [can] of milk which he had brought in from the outside safe [a place where food could be kept cold] .

The room swung back to its normal size as he sat down.

From 'Drifting' by Patricia Grace

a   List all the different aspects of the character's appearance described in the passage.
b   Is this a favourable description?
c   Why do you think the author describes the man in this way?
d   Now write a short paragraph describing the physical characteristics of either yourself or someone else. Be as positive as you can. Read over your work and decide what would you have to change to make your description negative?

The character's speech

When you are looking at what a character says, you need to ask yourself what the character's speech tells you about him or her. Look at:

▶   how he/she speaks. Does he/she talk a lot, or very rarely?
▶   whether he/she shouts, or speaks in a quiet manner.
▶   the type of sentences he/she uses. Are they short and abrupt, or long and flowing?

ACTIVITY 3

Read the following passage. Billy has just arrived home from his early morning paper round to find his mother getting ready for work.

'Oh, it's you Billy. Haven't you gone to school yet?'

'Who's that bloke?'

His mother pressed her lips together and stood the capsule [a lipstick], like a bullet, on the mantelpiece.

'That's Reg. You know Reg, don't you?'

She took a cigarette packet from the mantelpiece and shook it.

'Hell, I forgot to ask him for one.'

She dropped the packet into the hearth and turned to Billy.

'You haven't got a fag on you, love?'

. . . 'Is that him you came home wi' last night?'

'There's some tea mashed if you want a cup, but I don't know if t'milk's come or not.'

'Was it?'

'Oh stop pestering me! I'm late enough as it is.'

She crumpled her sweater into a tyre and eased her head through the hole, trying to prevent her hair from touching the sides.

'Do me a favour, love, run up to t'shop for some fags.'

'They'll not be open yet . . . I can't. I'll be late.'

'Go on, love, and bring back a few things wi' you; a loaf and some butter; and a few eggs, summat like that.'

'Go your sen.' [self]

From *A Kestrel for a Knave* by Barry Hines

Answer the following questions. They will help you to understand the relationship between the two characters more fully.

a   What do you notice about the way Billy talks to his mother?

b   What does she seem to want to avoid talking to him about?

c   How does she try to encourage Billy to do what she wants him to?

d   What sort of a relationship does Billy have with his mother?

e   How do you know the characters are speaking with an accent?

The character's actions

You should be aware of the things a character does. Consider:

▸   how he/she moves. Does he/she move quickly or slowly?

▸   what gestures or mannerisms he/she uses.

Remember to look out for any differences between the way a character acts and the things he/she says. Sometimes people can be saying one thing but their body language can be telling us something quite different. You should also be aware that sometimes a character can say very little. In this case you must pay particular attention to his/her actions, as this is your only way of finding out what he/she is really like.

ACTIVITY 4

Read the next passage carefully. It describes a schoolmaster called Waldo who teaches in an all boys' school.

Waldo's entrance to the classroom was theatrical. He strode in with strides as long as his soutane [gown] would permit, his books clenched in his left hand and pressed tightly against his chest. With his right hand he swung the door behind him, closing it with a crash. His eyes raked the class. If, as occasionally happened, it did not close properly he did not turn from the class but backed slowly against the door, snapping it shut with his behind. Two strides brought him to the rostrum. He cracked his books down with an explosion.

Waldo was very tall . . . His face was sallow and immobile. (There was a rumour that he had a glass eye but no one knew which. Nobody could look at him long enough because to meet his stare was to invite question.) He abhorred slovenliness [hated untidiness]. Once when presented with an untidy exercise book, dog-eared with a tea ring on the cover, he picked it up, the corner of one leaf between his finger and his thumb . . . opened the window and dropped it three floors to the ground.

From 'The Secret' by Bernard MacLaverty

Now answer these questions:

a   What are we told about how Waldo enters the classroom?
b   Why do you think the boys avoid making eye contact with Waldo?
c   What impression do you get of Waldo when you are told about how he throws the book out of the window?

The character's thoughts

A writer may choose to allow us to get to know a character better by providing us with an insight into his/her thoughts. Often this happens when the author is writing in the first person ('I'). Alternatively, a writer may prefer to adopt the stance of an all-seeing narrator who can inform us of what one or more of the characters are thinking.

Another technique writers sometimes use to allow us to get a better understanding of a character is called an **internal monologue**.

ACTIVITY 5

In the following passage we get an insight into the thoughts of a serial killer who is preying upon young homeless people. Read it and consider the questions that follow.

I've been out tonight. I took the tube down to Charing Cross and walked about a bit. Tour of inspection, you might say. And I found them, as I'd known I would. Hundreds of the scruffy blighters, lying around making the place look manky. I marched along the Strand and they were there dossing, in doorways . . . One cheeky bugger – couldn't have been more than seventeen – actually asked me for money. 'Have you got any change?' he says. I looked him up and down and I said, 'Change? I'd change you, my lad, if I had you in khaki for six weeks.' It didn't go in though. He just smiled and said have a nice night.

From 'Stone Cold' by Robert Swindells

a   Look at the character's language. Make a note of all the military phrases or references made. What does this suggest about his character?
b   What is his attitude towards the homeless?
c   Try rewriting this passage in the third person ('he'), without knowing what the character is thinking. What differences do you notice between the original version and your own?

Other characters' reactions

When you are trying to discover what a character is really like, it is important to look carefully at how other characters react to the person in whom you are interested. Consider whether:

▸ the other characters seem nervous around this person
▸ they enjoy the person's company.

ACTIVITY 6

Now read the following passage in which Angus's father comes to visit. Consider the questions that follow.

Angus had just finished wiping the walls and was reaching for the dishwasher for Leo's lunchbox when he heard a high-pitched voice behind him.

'Avast there, me hearty.'

He looked round.

A cloth hand-puppet that looked sort of like a pirate was poking around the kitchen door.

'I'm Pirate Jim,' said the voice. 'Splice me mainbrace and always wash your hands before meals.'

'Hi Dad,' said Angus wearily.

Dad came in grinning broadly and waggling the Pirate puppet in his hand. 'What do you reckon?' he said.

'Kids' TV show?' asked Angus hopefully. Dad needed a career break.

Dad frowned under his curls. 'That hopeless agent of mine couldn't get me a role in a bread shop,' he said, 'let alone in a TV show.' Then he grinned again, 'So . . . I'm writing a kids' book, Pirate Jim. I got the idea from when you told me you persuaded your teacher to do a school play about pirates.'

Angus stared at him, 'Dad, you're an actor not a writer.'

'Loads of actors write when they are between jobs . . .'

Angus suddenly found it hard to look at Dad.

From *Bumface* by Morris Gleitzman

a Is Angus happy to see his father? Choose words or phrases from the passage to support your answer.

b How does Angus react to his father's news of his new job?

c Why do you think Angus reacts to his father in this way?

Other characters' comments

To really understand what a character is like, it is also important to look at how other characters respond and react to them. It is worth remembering that it is not always wise to believe these comments – the other character making them might be biased!

ACTIVITY 7

In the following extract Judith Hearne is about to visit some friends called the O'Neills.

Read the passage carefully, paying particular attention to what the other characters say about Judith Hearne before she finally arrives.

At a quarter to three, Shaun O'Neill and I looked out of the drawing room window and saw Miss Hearne coming up the avenue.

'Daddy,' he said, 'J.H. sighted on the horizon. Prepare to abandon ship.'

His father nodded, picked up his newspaper and made for the door.

'I'll be in the study if you want me,' he said to his wife.

'Una and Kathleen. It's your turn to stay,' Moira O'Neill said. 'And I don't want any arguments about it.'

'But I have to prepare my stuff for tomorrow's lecture,' Una said.

'No. When you went to the dance last night, you told me you'd stay in today. I want you here. After all, poor Judy looks forward to seeing you. It's the big event of her week, the poor soul, and I'm not going to have her snubbed by you children.'

'Anyway, I'm off,' Shaun said. 'I've done my sentence.'

'Go on then. But I don't want any more jokes about this,' Mrs O'Neill said sternly. 'Kevin, you stay here.'

'O, holy smoke!' Kevin wailed.

'There she is,' Shaun said as the bell shrilled below in the hall.

Una, Kathleen and Kevin pulled long faces.

From *The Lonely Passion of Judith Hearne* by Brian Moore

a How do the family react when Miss Hearne is sighted walking up the avenue? What does this suggest about their feelings for her?

b 'It's your turn to stay... And I don't want any arguments about it.' What does this remark suggest about the girls' attitude to Miss Hearne?

c 'I've done my sentence.' What do you think Shaun means by this?

d What impression do you have of Miss Hearne, based on the comments and reactions of the O'Neill family towards her?

ACTIVITY 8

Below is a typical example of the sort of question you could be asked about a character in the exam. Read it and the passage that follows.

What sort of a person is Miss Evans?

Miss Evans walked fast. She was a little woman, not much taller than Carrie, but she seemed strong as a railway porter, carrying their cases as if they weighed nothing. They stopped outside a grocery shop with the name SAMUEL ISAAC EVANS above the door and Miss Evans took a key from her bag. She said, 'There's a back way and you'll use that, of course, but we'll go through the front for once, as my brother's not here.'

The shop was dim and smelled mustily pleasant. Candles and tarred kindling, and spices, Carrie thought, wrinkling her nose. A door at the back led into a small room with a huge desk almost filling it. 'My brother's office,' Miss Evans said in a hushed voice and hurried them through into a narrow dark hall with closed doors and a stair rising up. It was darker here than the shop and there was a strong smell of polish.

Polished linoleum, a shining glass sea, with rugs scattered like islands. Not a speck of dust anywhere. Miss Evans looked down at her feet. 'Better change into your slippers before we go up to your bedroom.'

'We haven't got any,' Carrie said. She meant to explain that there hadn't been any room in their cases but they could not speak before Miss Evans turned bright red and said quickly, 'Oh, I'm so sorry, how silly of me. Why should you? Never mind, as long as you are careful and tread on the drugget [a coarse woollen floor covering].'

. . . 'Call me Auntie,' Miss Evans said, 'Auntie Louise. Or Auntie Lou, if that's easier. But you'd best call my brother Mr Evans. You see, he's a councillor.' She paused and then went on in the same proud tone she had used when she showed them the bathroom, 'Mr Evans is a very important man. He's at a council meeting just now. I think I'd best give you your supper before he comes back, hadn't I?'

They had a good supper of eggs and milk and crunchy, fresh bread in the kitchen which was as clean as the rest of the house but more cheerful, with a big range fire that threw out heat like a furnace. Miss Evans didn't eat with them but stood by the table like a waitress in a restaurant, taking the plates and sweeping up crumbs around their chairs before they finished drinking their milk. She didn't actually say, 'Please hurry up, oh please hurry up,' but she might just as well have done; her mouth twitched as if she was muttering it inwardly, her eyes kept darting up to the clock on the mantelpiece and there were red nervous spots on her cheeks.

She made the children very nervous too. When she said, 'What about bed, now?' they were more than glad to escape from the kitchen where the Very Important Councillor Evans might appear any minute. As they went upstairs Miss Evans rolled the drugget up behind them. 'Mr Evans doesn't like to see it down,' she explained when she caught Carrie's eye. 'I just put it there while he's out, to keep the carpet spick and span. It's a new one, you see, lovely deep pile, and Mr Evans doesn't want it trodden on.'

. . . 'But the bathroom's upstairs,' Nick said in an outraged voice.

She looked at him apologetically. 'Yes, I know dear. But if you want to – you know – go anywhere, there's one at the end of the yard. Mr Evans doesn't use it, of course. It wouldn't be dignified for a man in his position, when all the neighbours know he's got one indoors, but I use it, and though it's an earth closet it's quite nice and clean.'

. . . A door banged downstairs. Nick looked at Carrie with eyes like black pits. 'Oh,' he said, 'Carrie. . .'

'Into bed now,' Miss Evans said, hustling past her. Then she began scuttling backwards and forwards like a small, frightened mouse, picking up the things they had dropped, clothes in the bedroom, toothpaste tube in the bathroom. 'Oh dear,' she was saying, under her breath, 'Oh dear, oh dear, oh dear. . .'

From *Carrie's War* by Nina Bawden

Before you answer this question let's look closely at it again in order to work out what it requires you to do.

What sort of a person is Miss Evans?

First, you need to consider the following.

▸ What are we told of her physical appearance? Does this suggest anything about her character?

▸ What does she say? Look especially at the way she talks about her brother.

▸ What does she do? Do her actions suggest anything about the type of person she is, or her relationship with her brother?

▸ What does she think? Does the third person narration allow us an insight into her thoughts? If not, how would such an insight change our opinion of Miss Evans?

▸ How do Nick and Carrie react to Miss Evans?

Now write your answer. Remember to support any comments you make with evidence from the passage.

Answering effectively

You will not have a long time to answer this question in the exam; you will need to get your points down quickly. This is best achieved by employing a deliberate style of answering. Use short paragraphs in which you make a judgement that you back up with evidence from the passage.

What follows is a straightforward example of what is not effective and what is. Here is what not to do:

✗ *Norma is good to her sister.*

It is probable that the writer of this answer was aware of the evidence. After all, an appropriate conclusion about the character has been made. But this has been done without presenting any proof, and consequently it will not attract as many marks as the following answer would.

✓ *We learn that Norma is kind and thoughtful because she is prepared to give her younger sister the chance to go on the trip although she won the prize.*

The conclusion is expressed clearly and the evidence to support it is summarised economically. You will note that it is not necessary to copy out the relevant chunk of text – this would simply be a waste of valuable time. Having completed this point, take a new paragraph and repeat the process, making your next point!

3 Understanding and using an empathy-based approach

Empathy is the imaginative process that allows us to sense what it is like to be another person. Through using our sense of empathy we can see, feel and experience the thoughts and emotions of that person. When it is used during reading, it permits us to climb inside a character and view the world through his/her eyes.

What's required?

You will be asked to employ your ability to imaginatively become one of the characters. By presenting a convincing view of the world from the character's viewpoint, you are demonstrating:

▸ your grasp of that character
▸ an awareness of the situation he/she is in
▸ an understanding of the relationships within the story.

The type of response that you will be asked to use will take the form of either a diary entry or a letter to a close friend or relative. Before you can begin to write either of these, it is vital that you have a real sense of the character whose viewpoint you have been asked to adopt. It stands to reason that only then will you be ready to present that individual's perspective.

The features of this type of writing

The characteristics of these diaries and personal letters are that:

▸ both are written using the first person ('I')
▸ they look back on a situation or incident
▸ both reflect upon the situation in an open and honest way
▸ the tone of the writing will reflect the character's mood and state of mind
▸ they will carefully mirror the attitude towards other characters, and the reaction to the situation of the chosen character, as it is presented in the story.

Four examples of writing based on empathy

ACTIVITY 9

Here's an example from a well-known diary. As you read it over, think about what you learn about the character and his attitudes.

Sue Townsend, the writer, has created the fictional young teenager Adrian Mole. This is one of 'his' diary entries. Nigel is his best friend and Pandora is a girl from his class. He worships her from a distance.

Monday January 19th

I have joined a group at school called the Good Samaritans. We go out into the community helping and stuff like that. We miss Maths on Monday afternoons.

Today we had a talk on the sort of things we will be doing. I have been put in the old age pensioners' group. Nigel has got a dead yukky job looking after kids in a playgroup. He is as sick as a parrot.

I can't wait for next Monday. I will get a cassette so I can tape all the old fogies' stories about the war and stuff. I hope I get one with a good memory.

The dog is back at the vet's. It has got concrete stuck on its paws. No wonder it was making such a row on the stairs last night. Pandora smiled at me in school dinner today, but I was choking on a piece of gristle so I couldn't smile back. Just my luck!

From *The Secret Diary of Adrian Mole Aged 13¾* by Sue Townsend

You will notice immediately that the style of this type of writing is frank and honest. It is almost as if Adrian has come home and is gossiping to a close friend about the highs and lows of his school day. As the audience for his diary entry is really only himself, the character is being completely open and so it very accurately reflects the young, immature teenager's concerns and attitudes.

What have we learnt about him?

▶ He has only a very general idea of what these 'Good Samaritans' actually do.

▶ We suspect his interest has much to do with the fact that he is missing Maths on a Monday afternoon.

▶ He seems to be rather smug about the fact that Nigel has been assigned to 'a dead yukky job' that he doesn't like. This appears to be more important than any real interest in the activity that he has been given.

▶ His comment about 'old fogies...with a good memory' is darkly humorous in its lack of sensitivity. It displays a lack of genuine concern and suggests a rather naïve outlook.

▶ The final paragraph is again comical as we hear details about his eccentric home life and an opportunity missed with Pandora.

ACTIVITY 10

Below is a different diary entry; it is taken from the real diary of Alan Bennett, the writer. It contrasts with Adrian's diary entry – it is much more serious and thoughtful.

In this entry Bennett notes his feelings after having left his ageing mother at her nursing home.

7 July 1981.

When I say goodbye to Mam after taking her back to the home at Weston, she gets out of the car saying, 'Thank you for all you've done for me, love.' And she means this; it isn't a remark intended to induce guilt. But in a film the next shot would be me looking down at the shaft of a spear protruding from my belly with the head stuck out a foot behind me.

From *Writing Home* by Alan Bennett

Although the tone and content are very different, like the diary entry from *Adrian Mole*, the same frank and honest approach makes this interesting.

What does this brief entry reveal about the character of its writer? We are left with the following impressions:

▸ The writer is a thoughtful and sensitive man who is close to his 'Mam'.
▸ He is deeply affected by her sincere words of thanks.

ACTIVITY 11

The next piece of writing is an example of a very lively personal letter from a young teenage girl.

Steve Skidmore and Steve Barlow, the writers, have created a fictional teenage girl called Sammy. She is writing to her friend, Camille, taking the opportunity to keep her up to date on all the latest gossip about the new term at school and her boyfriend Michael. . .

September 6th

Dear Camille,

Summer holidays ought to be three months long; six weeks is hopeless. You spend the first three weeks recovering from school and the last three dreading going back — where's the holiday in that?

It's all so depressing when you walk in through the door and it's just as if you'd never been away. Adolf, our head, looked as gruesome as ever — Michael reckoned he'd spent his holidays in the lab getting a new bolt put in his neck! But if we thought Adolf was The Creature from the Pit, that's only because we hadn't seen our new form teacher.

Where do they dredge them up from? ... Not that she LOOKS horrible – in fact, when she came in through the door for the first time, Michael sat up in his chair and started fiddling with his tie. 'Hello,' I thought, 'that's enough of that.' But to be fair, all the other boys in the class were tucking their shirts in and smoothing their hair as well.

Honestly, aren't men pathetic? The school spends a fortune on Equal Opportunities programmes and non-sexist encounter groups for them, and the minute they see any female who's half good-looking, they all put on sickly grins and start drooling.

I'm making her sound like a film star – she's not like that – it's just that you couldn't imagine her ever laddering her tights. Junket, who teaches us English, always looks as if she's got dressed in the dark during an earthquake wearing gardening gloves but this new woman is the opposite: everything about her is so neat and so clean it makes your teeth ache.

She wrote her name on the board, Ms Staines. Michael's hand was up like a shot. Was that short for Miss or Mrs? She gave him a frosty look and told him it was short for Ms. I was kicking him under the table, but Michael never knows when to shut up. He meant, was she married? With a glare that could have frozen hydrogen, she told him that wasn't his business. Everyone else was sniggering and I was scarlet with shame. Michael shut up, except for muttering under his breath things like 'sarky dragon' and 'I only ASKED' ...

I had a look round while she was taking the register; Zoe looked as if she was chewing a lemon ... Pitiful, really. Jealousy's a terrible thing.

Anyway, it turns out she's teaching us General Science as well as being our form teacher. All the lads looked dead pleased except Michael who mumbled something about 'Just our naffin' luck' – Staines heard him and made him clean the board for muttering. He sulked and took ages, but then when he'd finished and Staines said, 'Thank you, Michael', he grinned like an idiot, and if he'd had a tail he'd have thumped it on the floor. I can see I shall have to watch him ...

We're doing spreadsheets in Information Technology this term, so send me a list of your fellas and I'll see if the computer can keep tabs on them better than I can.

Love,

Sammy

From *In Love with an Urban Gorilla: Recycled Confessions* by Steve Skidmore and Steve Barlow

What does this letter tell us about Sammy? We learn that she:

▸ dislikes school
▸ has an unusual way of looking at things – her view of the school holidays
▸ has no sense of respect for her principal, Adolf
▸ is unimpressed by her boyfriend's reaction to Ms Staines
▸ sees Zoe as jealous, but does not recognise it in herself
▸ has a lively sense of humour – the idea of Michael's tail thumping on the ground.

ACTIVITY 12

The famous writer Roald Dahl offers a slightly different example of a personal letter.

After an almost fatal plane crash during the Second World War, he writes home to his mother describing his condition.

Alexandria 6 December 1940

Dear Mama,

I haven't written to you since my one and only letter some weeks ago, chiefly because the doctors said that it wasn't good for me. As a matter of fact I've been progressing very slowly. As I told you in my telegram I did start getting up, but they soon popped me back to bed again because I got such terrific headaches. A week ago I was moved back into this private room, and I have just completed a whole long 7 days lying flat on my back in semi darkness doing absolutely nothing – not even allowed to lift a finger to wash myself. Well, that's over, and I'm sitting up today, (it's eight o'clock in the evening actually) and writing this and incidentally feeling fine ... You needn't be alarmed – there's nothing very wrong with me, I've merely had an extremely serious concussion. They say I certainly won't fly for about six months, and last week were going to invalid me home on the next convoy. But somehow I didn't want to – once invalided home, I knew I'd never get on to flying again, and who wants to be invalided home anyway?

From *Going Solo* by Roald Dahl

We learn quite a lot about the young injured pilot from his letter.

▸ He describes his situation in quite a matter-of-fact way.
▸ He is trying to reassure his mother that he is feeling better.
▸ He tells her 'there's nothing very wrong...I've merely had...'
▸ We can sense his love of flying, his determination and his thirst for adventure – 'once invalided...'

Employing empathy in your writing

When you are asked to write using empathy, there are a number of requirements that have to be met before you begin if you are to succeed in adopting the persona of one of the individuals in the story. You need to:

▸ have a firm grasp of the personality of your character
▸ assess their attitude to the other characters in the story
▸ understand the situation they are in
▸ recognise the significant details from within the story that will provide you with the basis of your piece of writing.

ACTIVITY 13

Only when you have worked your way through these factors are you in a position to begin to write a convincing letter or diary entry. Below is a typical example of this type of question. Read it and the story that follows.

> **Imagine you are the boy in the red jersey. Write your diary entry about Neilly and the day he climbed the fir tree.**

Neilly watched dreamily as the boy in the red jersey dropped from the big fir tree back on to the ground again. The rest of the boys gathered round, calling out questions, but Neilly didn't move. He stood with his hands behind his back, a look of sadness in his large hazel eyes.

The boy in the red jersey shook his head, obviously very thankful to be back on firm ground again.

'It's no good! Nobody'll ever be able to climb that tree.'

He was the third to have attempted it. Two of the others had already tried, but they also had failed. The boy in the red jersey had the name of being the best climber of them all, and now that the big fir had beaten him too, well it didn't seem much good for anyone else to try.

He shook his head again. 'Nobody'll ever be able to climb that tree. . .You might be able to get *past* that part all right, but you'd never be able to get down again. You'd be stuck up there all night. Isn't that right, Franky?'

All the boys walked backwards out into the field, staring upwards, until halfway up the tree, they could see the bare part like a faint magic girdle encircling the trunk. Here for a space of about six or seven feet the trunk was devoid of branches. The boys argued and shook their heads. No one took the slightest notice of little Neilly standing a few yards away.

There were three firs here on top of the hill. Like three monuments erected by some long-vanished race of giants, they towered up into the air, a landmark for miles around.

Neilly gave a faint shudder as he looked up into the fir. He felt so terribly small and insignificant beside this glowering monster. Neilly was a small slight lad of about nine. He was easily the youngest and smallest of the entire group. His legs and arms were slender as reeds, and he wore a pair of ponderous looking black boots – no stockings. His right boot was soaking wet, and smeared with pale, gluey mud. That was where he had nearly fallen into St Bridget's drain, about ten minutes ago. Everyone else had jumped it except him. Poor Neilly! How he wished he were a bit bigger, so that he could jump and climb as well as the other lads. It wasn't his fault that he was so small, but the rest of the boys didn't think of that. When they did anything that he couldn't, they just jeered at him, or worse even – ignored him altogether. Neilly suddenly became aware of his companions' glances.

The boy in the red jersey was pointing at him dramatically. 'There you are!' he shouted. 'I bet you Neilly could climb it though. Couldn't you, Neilly?'

'Ah, he can't even jump St Bridget's drain, yet, even,' another boy chimed in. At this Neilly bit his lip, hiding his wet, muddy boot behind his dry left one.

The boys came closer.

'Ah, poor wee Neilly! What are you blushing about, Neilly? What are you blushing about?'

The boy in the red jersey stuck his hands up.

'I still say that Neilly could climb that tree.' He put his hand on Neilly's shoulder. 'Couldn't you, Neilly?'

Neilly shook the hand off instantly. The boy gave him a push, and then the rest of the boys began pushing him too. Neilly became infuriated. He made a wild swing with his boot, but the boys only jeered louder. Neilly's rage increased. He broke through his tormentors, and rushed over to the fir.

'For two pins I would climb your ould tree for you,' he raged. 'D'you think I couldn't, like?'

The jeering grew louder. The boys were enjoying themselves immensely. With a mighty effort Neilly forced himself to be calm. He turned to the tree. The lower part of the enormous trunk was worn smooth and shiny, where the cows had come to scratch. Neilly stripped off his boots, then, standing on a great, hump-backed root, he gave a jump, reaching for a huge, rusty staple which was driven into the trunk about five feet off the ground.

He caught it, skinning his knee against the bark. He made another lunge towards the first branch a little higher, and drew himself up, casting a swift, triumphant glance at the boys below.

> *Neilly succeeded in climbing to the top of the tree. Although he slipped and nearly fell on his way down, he managed to make it safely back to the ground.*

...he at last dropped back on to solid earth, he was smiling, and his eyes shone. The instant he hit the ground again, the boys swarmed around, cheering and clapping him on the back. Neilly retreated a few steps, breathlessly.

'Good man, Neilly!' the boy in the red jersey was shouting. 'You did what nobody else here the day would have done. Boy-oh-boy when we seen you dropping down that bare part there, we sure thought you were a goner. Didn't we boys?'

'We sure did!' the rest of the boys chorused. 'That was powerful, Neilly ...'

The boys brought his boots over for him, and the boy in the red jersey cleaned his muddy one with grass.

As Neilly was sitting down putting on his boots, his trousers slipped up, and he was surprised to see a long red scratch on his leg. Then he remembered where he had slipped on his downward journey.

The boys all bent down to examine the wound, and then they began advising him to come home, and get some iodine on it. Neilly smiled. It was only a scratch really and not painful at all, but for some reason he felt terribly proud of it.

As the boys escorted him over the fields, home, he put on a slight limp, and every twenty yards or so, he would glance back at the middle fir that he'd climbed, and then down at his leg again, and then back to the fir again, and his eyes were shining with wonder, and joy.

From 'Neilly and the Fir Tree' by John O'Connor

Going about the business of answering this question

a   Let's look more closely at the question again in order to work out what it requires you to do.

Imagine you are the boy in the red jersey. *Write your diary entry about Neilly and the day he climbed the fir tree.*

The opening sentence of the question tells you whose viewpoint you are to use. Here you are to be 'the boy in the red jersey'. You are to view the events through the eyes of this character.

Imagine you are the boy in the red jersey. **Write your diary entry about Neilly and the day he climbed the fir tree.**

The second sentence of the question tells you exactly what you have to do – write a diary entry – and what it has to be about – Neilly and what he did that day.

b   The next thing to do is to discover what we learn about the boy in the red jersey and his attitude to Neilly in the first section of the story. Use evidence from the opening section of the story to answer the questions below. This will help you sort out your ideas about him.

   ▸ What role does the boy in the red jersey have within the group?

   ▸ Does he seriously think the small boy can climb the tree?

   ▸ How does he treat Neilly when he turns his attention to the small boy?

   ▸ What do the other boys think of Neilly?

   ▸ How would you sum up his attitude and behaviour towards Neilly before he starts his climb?

Having worked your way through these points, you now have a much clearer idea of what he thought about Neilly before the tree climbing.

c   Now let's assess how Neilly is treated after he has completed his successful climb. Again, use the following questions to help you think about this section of the story.

   ▸ How does the gang greet him when he reaches the ground?

   ▸ How would you sum up the remarks offered by the boy in the red jersey?

   ▸ What do these comments tell us about his attitude to Neilly now?

   ▸ Sum up the way Neilly is treated as the group of boys walk away from the fir tree.

d   Before you begin to write your answer, there is one final consideration. What are the main events around which your diary entry will be based? In the case of this story, they are:

   ▸ the failures, including your own, to climb the tree

   ▸ poking fun at Neilly with the assistance of the others

   ▸ Neilly's angry, childish reaction to the teasing

   ▸ his decision to attempt to climb the tree

   ▸ his success where you had failed

   ▸ the reception he receives from you and the others when he is down safely.

These points could usefully offer you the paragraph headings around which you will write your diary account. You are ready to begin, but before you do so read this important final section.

Answering effectively

Remember the examiner wants you to include your **thoughts** and **feelings** about the changes in attitude towards Neilly. If you ignore this you are failing to meet the most important requirement of the question: to show an in-depth understanding of the characters and their situation.

Here are some final reminders about the writing of letters and diary entries.

▶ Write in the first-person ('I').

▶ Use a writing style (the sort of words and phrases) that you consider would be appropriate to your character. Remember, a diary entry looks back on a day's events picking out highlights and recording the writer's thoughts and feelings about what happened. A letter can serve a series of purposes, but it is probable that you will be required to share a problem/discuss a dilemma with a friend.

▶ You will still have to maintain the character's persona and show a clear understanding of his/her situation.

▶ Present thoughts and feelings that are appropriate and demonstrate an understanding of the character.

▶ Make use of details from the story to develop a convincing response.

▶ Do not simply retell the story.

4 Looking at setting

You may be asked a question that focuses on setting. By this we mean the location and surroundings in which the story takes place. This type of question will look at the way in which the setting or location can assist with creating a particular mood or atmosphere.

What's required?

You will be expected to show an understanding of the ways in which the setting for the story has been developed.

The reader is presented with setting through:

▶ the nature of the surroundings. The writer might choose any of the following types of location – pleasant, tranquil, bland, dramatic, threatening, menacing or hostile.

▶ the description of the surroundings and the writer's particular selection of language.

▶ the reactions of the characters to their surroundings.

When reading fiction you need to be aware of these and the effect they have. You also need to remember that all of the information is coming directly to you from one person – the author. The author is guiding and influencing your response to the setting.

The easiest way to demonstrate the effect of setting is by looking at some examples and working through them.

ACTIVITY 14

Read the following excerpt. It presents comments that will help you to understand how the writer uses the setting to:

▸ reflect the sense of unease felt by the characters

▸ create an increasingly tense situation.

Four young people with a shared interest in animal rights are going on a night raid on a puppy farm.

Notice how the character's nervousness is reflected through the use of the simile 'like monsters from a nightmare'. The use of 'leaned over', 'leering' and 'creaking' further add to the threatening feel of the surroundings.

They were well away from the town now. Elaine shivered slightly as the car's headlights illuminated the old trees and hedgerows so that they looked like monsters from a nightmare as they leaned over the Mini, leering and creaking in the wind.

'Park about half a mile further up the lane and we'll walk back,' Steve suggested. 'There's a gateway. A bit risky to park any closer, like we did last week.'

They piled out. Karen handed Mike his camera. It looked impressive with its various attachments.

'Got the torches?' Karen asked Steve.

'Yes. You carry one and I'll take the other. Keep them off for the moment though – the moon will give us enough light.'

Mike locked the car and gave Elaine's arm a reassuring squeeze. She smiled back gratefully and followed the others. They hurried along the lane, the farm buildings standing out black against the moonlit sky. The windows of the derelict farmhouse stared like unwinking eyes, so that Elaine gave a sudden shiver. All those half-remembered ghost stories came back to haunt her and her instincts told her to run away – NOW!

A heavy iron gate barred the way at the farm entrance but beside it there was a narrow gap in the wall. Steve led the way and he paused to survey the quiet buildings before signalling the 'all-clear'.

'No one around. Come on – there's no law against going for a walk. . .even if it's night-time!'

'Is that where the animals are?' Elaine asked. She pointed towards the huge, black barn, beyond the pond.

'No, that's where they store hay and straw.' Steve pointed towards a long, low building near the farmhouse. 'That's it – over there.'

They crossed the yard in front of the accusing stare of the black farmhouse windows. Suddenly they heard a noise which stopped them in their tracks. Over to the right there was a muffled growling and barking.

The sense of uneasiness that the characters are experiencing is reinforced by the writer's repetition of the earlier image of the staring windows. This time she uses the adjective 'accusing' to develop their sense of nervousness. The windows are again described using the adjective 'black' to imply menace.

The 'buildings standing out black' adds to the sense of danger and threat. The windows 'stared' — here the writer uses a metaphor (personification) to emphasise the sense of threat. This is continued with the simile 'like unwinking eyes'.

It is also interesting to note the character's reaction to the scene — ghost stories return to haunt her. The sense of personal threat is such that she wants to run. Note the use of block capitals to emphasise her desire to flee.

continued

'Darn!' Steve groaned. 'There were no guard dogs here last week. The farm bloke took them away with him, two of them.'

'Sounds as though they're shut up, over there.' Karen nodded towards a tractor shed.

'D'you think anyone will hear them?' Elaine asked anxiously.

'Shouldn't think so, not in this wind. Anyway, they'll soon stop.'

Steve walked on and the others followed, looking edgy.

From 'Run with the Hare' by Linda Newbery

ACTIVITY 15

Read the following passage. The question focuses on how the writer uses setting to build up mood and atmosphere.

How does the setting add to the tension that Sonny is feeling?

Father Pestle steeled himself and played the man. He took Sonny gently by one shoulder and said kindly, 'Let's go into church for a minute.' Though he trembled and prayed desperately for a strength and clear sight he knew he did not have.

To Sonny, his hand was a policeman's hand. More, the hand of God himself. Like a condemned murderer, he let himself be led to trial and execution. It was a relief, really. How had he ever thought he could get away with it? God knew every step he took. . .

They were in the church now; in the dark. Only the huge pointed blue windows gave a dim light, and within that light, the walls of Jericho fell and tumbled for ever, and God turned Lot's wife to a pillar of salt, and the saints and prophets turned their terrible bearded faces to look at Sonny as he passed. And, even dimmer in the darkness, the life-size angels glimmered their white robes and gold wings and cold uncaring faces. The whole court of Heaven was assembled for the trial, and now he was led to the feet of the Judge, the awful judge who hung in agony on the Cross, the blood oozing from his gaping wounds in round red blobs.

Father Pestle sat with a leathery creak, and forced Sonny down beside him. Sonny's one thought was of Mam. Somewhere, he thought, in the back corridors of Heaven, Mam must be struggling to reach him, defend him. But what was Mam in comparison to the saints and angels? They would never let her through in time; they would not listen to her. . .But he said, as if with his last breath (for it had become very difficult to breathe):

'Mam!'

From *A Time of Fire* by Robert Westall

Thinking about the question

We are being asked about setting so in rereading the passage we need to think about the relevant evidence that builds that tension.

Look at these points – they will lead you through the evidence offered in the passage.

▸ The tension is there right from the start and both the priest and Sonny feel it.

▸ Such is the boy's sense of guilt that the hand on Sonny's shoulder very quickly develops in the boy's imagination from 'a policeman's hand' to 'the hand of God himself'. Sonny sees himself as a 'condemned murderer'.

▸ Going into the church is like being 'led to trial and execution' and 'God knew every step he took'.

▸ Inside the church is 'dark', which further adds to the boy's uneasiness.

▸ Things are huge in comparison to the boy – 'the huge pointed blue windows'.

▸ The biblical stories are of terrible justice being handed out.

▸ The statues of the saints and prophets look down with 'terrible bearded faces'.

▸ The darkness increases as does the boy's sense of guilt.

▸ The angels have 'cold uncaring faces'.

▸ The writer reintroduces the theme of being in court and on trial – 'The whole court of Heaven was assembled for the trial'.

▸ Jesus is the 'awful judge'.

▸ Sonny is so completely overcome as he imagines his 'Mam' struggling in vain to come to his defence that he can hardly breathe.

ACTIVITY 16

Read this passage. Think about the significance of the setting. Consider the sections in red and assess their importance in the development of the setting.

Martin and Sean are two bored teenagers on their summer holidays, complaining that there is nothing to do. Dramatically, things change and they find themselves acting as guides for the police who are involved in a manhunt. The Clough, where the search is taking place, is a dome-shaped, desolate upland area. Greeny is one of the policemen.

Suddenly they all stopped. The Alsatian sniffed back and forth, back and forth across the path. It began to wag its big feathery tail. Sean's mouth went dry. Martin looked at him. The slow, happy, sinister tail of the dog and its snuffling muzzle struck coldness in both of them. Unexpected. Real. And the night tightened one more turn. They were all frozen, poised, watching the lowered snout, the black wagging tail. The silence was like a shout.

Then the dog trotted on, patient on the leash, and its handler shrugged. A false alarm. They climbed on. Martin kept by Sean's side now. They went slower.

Two ewes, startled, pranced to their feet from under the wall. They stared at the strangers with their goatish eyes, then bounded away. The bracken cracked and rustled as they vanished. The dog hardly looked at them. It was trained to hunt men.

Now they were moving above the bracken, under the screes, where once a great glacier had ground out the edge. There were boulders here, all shapes and sizes. And every boulder seemed to have eyes and a gun. If you looked at a stone too long in the darkness it seemed to move, to shimmer and tremble, like a man crouching. And now there were no walls to keep to, or duck behind. It was hard to imagine the other search parties less than a mile away on Clough Top, or Widow's Jump. They seemed so alone. Even in daylight the Clough always got bigger as you climbed it.

'Where's this shaft then?' Greeny asked.

Martin stopped. 'We must have passed it.'

Sean could see him frowning, trying to get his bearings. 'We'd have seen,' said Sean thoughtfully, 'if someone had gone through the bracken today. They'd have flattened a path.'

'Thank you, Sherlock,' said Greeny in that hard voice.

'Come on. We'll have to double back. Lead on, Macduff.'

Now Martin was up in front with the dog as they crab-crawled sideways and down on the flank of the Clough. Sean trailed behind, angry. It isn't 'Lead on, Macduff,' he thought over and over, staring at the black, broad back of the sergeant. It's 'Lay on, Macduff, and damn'd be him that first cries Hold, enough!' They were doing *Macbeth* in English. He had begun to hate Greeny, with his hard, clever voice. And he hated the piggy whistle of the man's breath as he clambered along in front of him.

'Down there,' Martin said, pointing. Then a great blue flicker lit the fell side, and they saw everything in strobe-light, so that the after-image stuck on their eyes like a photograph. They blinked darkness. No thunder came. Then another sheet of lightning shocked the sky, and an imprint of everything they saw stayed with them.

The mouth of the old mine, blue and grey and black, with the fence-posts and barbed wire, was twenty feet below them. The wire was twisted and down. The posts askew. They blinked in the after-blindness of the electric storm – but all of them had seen. A section of wire was twisted and crushed down – big enough to let a man through.

From 'Reiker', *Badger on the Barge* by Janni Howker

ACTIVITY 17

Read this next excerpt. It is the opening of a book entitled *Whispers in the Graveyard*.

My footprints track across the faint dew still lying on the grass. My boots crunch heavily on the hard gravel path, and I'm talking to myself as I walk, school bag bumping on my back. But the residents lodged on either side of these avenues won't complain about the noise.

They're dead.

Every one of them.

Their headstones march beside me. I stop to look at one of my favourites. A weaver. There is a carving of a leopard with a shuttle in its mouth. The animal's head is black with age, its stone roar a silent echo in a grey Scottish kirkyard. The leopard used to be on the crest of the Guild of Weavers. My dad told me.

Early morning mist comes creeping between the gravestones. I shiver. It's because I'm cold though, not scared.

Not yet.

I touch the old tinker's grave. A ram's horns and crossed spoons. That's how I know a tinker is buried there. The carvings and designs on the stones tell you. They all mean something. My dad told me to listen and I would hear the crackle of the gypsies' campfire, the black pot swinging just above the flames.

I wish words on paper were as easy to read and understand.

There's a big stone vase monument on this path, with a draped cloth and a trailing vine. That's a symbol from the Bible. Dad read out a psalm to me one night. 'Fruitful vine, and olive plants.' I liked the sound of those words, rolling around inside my head.

Masons used trees and plants a lot on memorials, ivy and bay leaf, lilies, thistles and roses. It's traditional. They used to strew flowers on graves in ancient times, and grow evergreens in kirkyards.

I leave the path and cross the grass past the pile of stones that make up the cairn memorial and go towards the back wall. It's empty and bare here. Only a single rowan tree growing, and just behind it the dyke is half broken down.

From *Whispers in the Graveyard* by Theresa Breslin

The title *Whispers in the Graveyard* is sinister to begin with, but how does the setting help to develop this sense of uneasiness? Consider:

▶ the location and manner in which it is revealed to us by the first person narrator
▶ the detailed descriptions
▶ how the narrator views the place
▶ the effect of particular words and phrases.

Answering effectively

You will not have a long time to answer this question in the exam so your answer needs to be to the point and economical. Answer purposefully. Use short paragraphs in which you refer to a significant piece of evidence from the passage and then explain its significance.

What follows is an instance of what is not effective and what is. This is what not to do.

> ✗ *We see the deserted countryside and town through the eyes of the main character: 'It didn't matter what I told myself, I simply couldn't shake off the sense that this was no normal Sunday.'*

The student writing this answer has a valid point to make. After all, he/she recognises the central point about how we are shown the setting. But this is not linked to the development of the setting or its effect. As a result it will not score as highly as the same point thoroughly tied into the question.

✓ *The writer has used the increasingly nervous outlook of her main character to build the reader's sense of unease. First, we are shown deserted countryside and then, even more worryingly, a deserted town. Our sense that something is fundamentally wrong grows as the mood of the heroine darkens: 'this was no normal Sunday'.*

This part of the answer is expressed clearly and the supporting evidence is presented economically. Notice that the use of quotation is kept to a minimum. Having made the analysis of this piece of evidence, take a new paragraph and move on to the next!

5 The writer's craft

In order to answer this type of question, one basic point has to be grasped. Unlike the two questions that have gone before, this one does not concern itself with the meaning – the outcome of the writing – but rather it focuses on **how** the writer has developed meaning. **How** that writer has built up a piece of text that has engaged you, the reader.

As soon as you read a text you are responding to a writer's craft. The writer has created the text and you, as a reader, respond to it. Meaning arises through the process of reading; meaning arises between the work of the writer in creating the text and you as a reader in responding to the text.

What's required?

You will be asked to consider and to write about how the author has stimulated your response through his/her methods in creating the text. Start with your own response and then consider how your response has arisen from the methods used by the writer. Such methods include:

▸ creating **beginnings** and **endings**
▸ developing **character**
▸ creating **setting** and **mood**
▸ making use of **language**.

Creating beginnings and endings

The examiner frequently uses the beginning of a literary text because this is the point at which the writer, in a concentrated manner, is establishing character, plot, setting and action. In the case of an ending, it is where the author is drawing all these elements together for a finale.

Beginnings

ACTIVITY 18

Read the following beginning to a story. Think through how the passage acts as a beginning. Consider what the author is leading you to expect, and how you as a reader are being encouraged to read on.

Gerry sat on JJ's windowsill with his head in his hands. It was no use. You could only search your pockets so many times. The money was gone; he'd lost it. There was no point in retracing his steps, either. English Ned had already made two sweeps of the street before shuffling down to the off-licence. Nope, if the cash had slipped out of Gerry's pocket, it had long since been converted into cider.

Things wouldn't have been so bad if it'd been his own money. Gerry snorted. Chance would be a fine thing. When was the last time he'd had his own money? It was Dad's cigarette money. And cigarettes were important to Dad. Since his back had given out, Dad said a nice fag with a cup of tea was one of the few pleasures he had left.

'Those fags will kill you,' Gerry had said.

Tom Coghlan had smiled a sad smile and said, 'They'll never get the chance, son.'

From 'Satellite Batteries' by Eoin Colfer

We are going to consider how this short extract works as a beginning to a story by asking and answering a series of questions.

a How does the author convey an impression of Gerry's circumstances and lifestyle?
  ‣ The early reference to 'JJ's windowsill' could imply a row of terraced houses, perhaps.
  ‣ The sweeping of the street by the cider-drinking 'English Ned' suggests that his surroundings are rather down at heel.
  ‣ The boy has no money of his own.

b How does the author convey an impression of the relationship between Gerry and his father?
  ‣ We gain our first insight before they come together at the end of the extract. The second paragraph is built around the boy's sense of regret and responsibility. The author permits Gerry a moment of self-pity – 'When was the last time he'd had his own money?' – but this is very quickly forgotten as the boy re-establishes what is important and why – the loss, by him, of his father's cigarette money.
  ‣ The piece of dialogue between the two characters is used by the writer to further confirm the boy's concern for his father – 'Those fags will kill you'.

c How does the author convey Gerry's state of mind?
  ‣ The author chooses to open the story in the middle of events. The money has already been lost and the author's opening sentence presents us with Gerry in what appears to be a state of distress. This is hinted at through the description of the boy's body language – sitting on a windowsill with 'his head in his hands'. The reader's initial suspicions are confirmed by the four-word sentence that follows.

▸ The main way that the author informs the reader of what the boy is thinking is by allowing us to share in his thoughts. This strategy is used from the second sentence of the opening paragraph.

▸ His mood – he is resigned to the loss of the money – is reinforced by the blunt sense of finality created by the short sentence that sums up the situation and his complete responsibility for the loss – 'The money was gone; he'd lost it.' This sense of resigned despair is sustained by the use of the words 'no point', 'Nope' and 'long since'.

d How does the author make the reader want to read on?

▸ The author invites a sense of empathy with Gerry – we've all lost things that are important to us, at one time or another.

▸ The father's final comment and 'sad smile' suggest intriguingly that something tragic might be about to happen and so our curiosity is aroused.

ACTIVITY 19

Read this opening to a story. Answer the questions that follow – they will help you to think through how the passage acts as a beginning.

'The minister, the Reverend Murdo Mackenzie, and his son Kenneth, will be visiting the school tomorrow,' Mr MacRea told the boys of Standard Seven. 'I want you to be on your best behaviour'. They sat two to a seat in a room which was white with the light of the snow.

'That is all I have to say about it,' he said. He unfurled a map which he stretched across the blackboard. 'And now,' he said, 'we will do some geography.'

The following day was again a dazzle of white. Mr MacRea took a watch from his breast pocket and said, 'They will be here at eleven o'clock. It is now five to eleven and time for your interval.' They rushed out into the playground and immediately began to throw snowballs at each other. They would perhaps have a longer interval today and then Mr MacRea would blow his whistle and they would form lines and march into the room.

Torquil shook his head as he received a snowball in the face and then ran after Daial, whom he hit with a beauty. The sky was clear and blue, and the snow crisp and fresh and white.

At eleven o'clock they saw a stout sombre man clad in black climb the icy steps to the playground, a small pale boy beside him. They stopped throwing snowballs for they knew this was the minister. He halted solidly in the middle of the playground and said, 'This is my son Kenneth. I shall leave him with you for a while. I am going to see Mr MacRea.'

He had a big red face and a white collar which cut into his thick red neck. Mr MacRea was waiting for him at the door and they saw him bend forward a little as he welcomed the minister into the school.

From 'Snowballs' by Iain Crichton Smith

a How does the author build up your image of the time and place in which the story is set?

b How does the author build up your expectations of what might happen next?

c How does the passage work as a beginning?

ACTIVITY 20

Read this opening to a story. Answer the questions that follow – they will help you to develop your ideas about the beginning of this story.

When we were children our father often worked on the night-shift. Once it was spring-time, and he used to arrive home, black and tired, just as we were downstairs in our nightdresses. Then night met morning face to face, and the contact was not always happy. Perhaps it was painful to my father to see us gaily entering upon the day into which he dragged himself soiled and weary. He didn't like going to bed in the spring morning sunshine.

But sometimes he was happy, because of his long walk through the dewy fields in the first daybreak. He loved the open morning, the crystal and the space, after a night down pit. He watched every bird, every stir in the trembling grass, answered the whinnying of the peewits, and tweeted to the wrens. If he could, he also would have whinnied and tweeted and whistled in a native language that wasn't human. He liked non-human things best.

One sunny morning we were all sitting at table when we heard his heavy slurring walk up the entry. We became uneasy. His was always a disturbing presence, trammelling. He passed the window darkly, and we heard him go into the scullery and put down his tin bottle, but directly he came into the kitchen we felt at once that he had something to communicate. No one spoke. We watched his black face for a second.

'Give me a drink,' he said.

From 'Adolf' by D.H. Lawrence

a How does the author use contrasts to convey the relationship between the father and the family?
b How does the author convey a sense of trouble to come?
c How does the passage work as a beginning?

Endings

ACTIVITY 21

Think through how this extract acts as a conclusion. Consider what the author is leaving you with, how you as a reader are affected and how that effect has been achieved.

Half a lap to go and Guaracara Park was a shouting, screaming din. Alvin Levis was half a bicycle ahead and Matthews was holding off Leon by half a wheel. Hackett the Whizz Wheeler slid back and there was nothing of Prestor at all. Leon set his teeth and ground and pounded and the blue Wasp began to sing. Matthews grimaced as Leon's front wheel gradually eased away from him. And now Leon was collaring Levis and the two bikes had drawn almost level.

Pandemonium broke loose and the crowd jumped the railings to race towards the finish line. The stewards fought and shouted to keep them from edging in on the track, the two cyclists hammered, Alvin Levis holding his own, and the shouting shook the place. Now they took the home straight. Leon's head hung forward and he pushed and pounded until the tissues of his belly felt as though they would be ripped away. He was in the very last of his strength. His face twisted in agony, and his lips were skinned and white with the dust and he rocked and jerked the bike, and now his tyre found a little edge in front, and as he struggled to maintain it, chaos broke over the grounds. The little boy clung to his father. The father's face was drenched with sweat and he was jumping and shouting. 'Now!' he cried, 'Now! N-Now!' and as the dust kicked, and the flag went up, he was overwhelmed and he wept.

From 'The Bicycle Race' by Michael Anthony

We are going to consider how this short extract works as a conclusion by asking and answering a series of questions.

a   How does the author convey the effort of the cyclists in the closing stages of the race?
  ▸ The sense of the effort being put in by the cyclists is conveyed through the large number of dramatic descriptions of their hard work – 'Leon set his teeth and ground and pounded', 'Matthews grimaced', 'the two cyclists hammered', 'Leon's head hung forward and he pushed and pounded. . .the tissues of his belly felt. . .they would be ripped away', 'in the very last of his strength', 'face twisted in agony' and 'his lips were skinned'.

b   How does the author convey the excitement and the atmosphere for the spectators in the final stages of the race?
  ▸ The description of Guaracara Park is expressed in terms of noise – 'a shouting, screaming din.'
  ▸ The writer divides his description between the excitement of the action on the track and the wildly excited reactions of the crowd as the race approaches its finish – 'Pandemonium broke loose', 'the crowd jumped the railings to race towards the finish line. The stewards fought and shouted'. The writer chooses to break away from the cyclists as they approach the finish line to describe the 'chaos' that 'broke over the grounds'. Our attention is focused on a child and his overwrought father who is yelling support, drenched in sweat and so overcome at the end of the race that 'he was overwhelmed and he wept.'

c   How does the passage work as an ending?
  ▸ The ending is certainly full of drama and suspense – even without having read the remainder of the story!
  ▸ It keeps the reader in a state of expectation until the final line.
  ▸ By concentrating on the reactions of the father and boy we share in the emotions of those most closely affected by the result.
  ▸ There is a clear sense that this is a gloriously happy ending – and we all enjoy it when things turn out as we hope they might.

ACTIVITY 22

Read this ending to a story. Answer the questions that follow.

Pigeon is the nickname given to a new boy, William, who has come to the narrator's school. He is bullied by Arthur Boocock and his gang because he has a strange accent and is Jewish.

Everything that had been happening with the Pigeon. It wasn't right. I knew it wasn't right and I decided. I wasn't going to be on Boocock's side.

I got to school early next morning and looked for him. He was at the bottom end of the playground on his own as usual. He was sitting on his bag, reading. My heart was thumping.

'Hi, William.'

He looked up, surprised.

'Hello.'

I fished out the bag of sweets I'd bought.

'Do you want a Nuttall's Minto?'

'Thank you. . .'

He was just going to take one but stopped. I could see him looking behind me. I turned round. Boocock, Barraclough, Norbert and Hopwood and a few others were coming towards us. My heart started thumping even more. He didn't say anything. He just stood staring at me.

'I'm not gonna be on your side, Arthur. I think it's stupid. I don't think we should have sides.'

I was still holding the bag of sweets. Boocock looked at me.

'Traitor!'

He would have hit me but William stepped in front and thumped him right in the stomach – hard. Boocock couldn't believe it. None of us could. He couldn't speak. I think it was 'cos he was winded but it might have been 'cos he was surprised, I wasn't sure. He got his mad up then and went for William – and William hit him again. Harder. I looked at Boocock lying on the ground, holding his stomach and crying. God had answered my prayers at last. Boocock was getting a taste of his own medicine. And all I could think was that it was a good job I *hadn't* prayed for anything bad to happen to him, like getting run over or getting ill.

William went back and sat on his bag and started reading again. I followed him.

'You're a good fighter, William.'

He looked up and smiled.

'My father says we must only use violence as a last resort. I think that was a last resort, don't you?'

I didn't know what he was talking about. I held out the bag of sweets.

'Here, have a Nuttall's Minto. . .'

From 'The Pigeon' by George Layton

a How does the writer's use of first-person narration help to create the excitement as this story reaches its end?

b How does the unexpected outcome of the story add to our enjoyment of it?

ACTIVITY 23

Read this ending to a novel. Answer the questions that follow.

Marty South and Mrs Grace Fitzpiers had both been romantically attached to Giles Winterborne. He is dead, and it is to his grave that the two women are meant to be going together.

That evening had been the particular one of the week upon which Grace and herself had been accustomed to privately deposit flowers on Giles's grave, and this was the first occasion since his death eight months earlier on which Grace had failed to keep her appointment. Marty had waited in the road just outside Melbury's, where her fellow-pilgrim had been wont to join her, till she was weary; and at last, thinking that Grace had missed her, and gone on alone, she followed the way to the church, but saw no Grace in front of her. It got later, and Marty continued her walk till she reached the churchyard gate: but still no Grace. Yet her sense of comradeship would not allow her to go on to the grave alone, and still thinking the delay had been unavoidable she stood there with her little basket of flowers in her clasped hands, and her feet chilled by the damp ground, till more than two hours had passed. She then heard the footsteps of Melbury's men . . . In the silence of the night Marty could not help hearing fragments of their conversation, from which she acquired a general idea of what had occurred, and that Mrs Fitzpiers was by that time in the arms of another man than Giles.

Immediately. . .she entered the churchyard, going to a secluded corner behind the bushes where rose the unadorned stone that marked the last bed of Giles Winterborne . . . She stooped down and cleared away the withered flowers that Grace and herself had laid there the previous week, and put her fresh ones in their place.

'Now, my own, own love,' she whispered, 'you are mine, and only mine: for she has forgot 'ee at last, although for her you died! But I – whenever I get up I'll think of 'ee, and whenever I lie down I'll think of 'ee again. Whenever I plant the young larches I'll think that none can plant as you planted; and whenever I split a gad [a wooden rod or stake], and whenever I turn the cider wring, I'll say none could do it like you. If ever I forget your name let me forget home and heaven! . . . But no, no, my love, I never can forget 'ee; for you was a good man, and did good things!'

From *The Woodlanders* by Thomas Hardy

a How does Hardy create a sympathetic picture of Marty?
b Look at the last paragraph in detail. Consider the way Hardy uses this simple countrywoman's dialect to create a moving and eloquent speech.

Developing character

This section will help you to explain how the writer has created the picture of a character in the text. Having read the text the reader should be able to identify the character type being presented. The character may be:

▶ a narrator or observer of events
▶ a hero/heroine

- ▶ a victim
- ▶ a villain
- ▶ a leader
- ▶ a bully
- ▶ a friend
- ▶ a relation.

The first topic this book considered was how the reader could understand character. Now we are looking at character from the other end, analysing what techniques may be used by a writer to construct character. These include:

- ▶ the viewpoint from which the events unfold. How is the story being narrated?
- ▶ words/phrases chosen to describe appearance, behaviour, emotion, actions and relationships with others.
- ▶ varieties of sentence types to help the reader build up an impression of meaning.
- ▶ use of dialogue, dialect/accent, speech, verbs and adverbs.

ACTIVITY 24

This sounds quite difficult when considered as theory. Let's look at how this works with a text.

In the extract below, the writer introduces the reader to the character of Gandalf for the first time in the story. The text has been annotated to highlight the techniques used by the author to build up the picture.

> Long opening sentence to build up dramatic arrival of central character. Short exclamation follows.

By some curious chance one morning long ago in the quiet of the world, when there was less noise and more green, and the hobbits were still numerous and prosperous, and Bilbo Baggins was standing at his door after breakfast, smoking an enormous long wooden pipe that reached nearly down to his woolly toes (neatly brushed) – Gandalf came by. Gandalf! If you had heard only a quarter of what <u>I</u> have heard about him, and I have only heard very little of all there is to hear, you would be prepared for any sort of remarkable tale. Tales and adventures sprouted up all over the place wherever he went, in the most extraordinary fashion. He had not been down that way under The Hill for ages and ages, not since his friend the Old Took died, in fact, and the hobbits had almost forgotten what he looked like. He had been away over The Hill and across The Water on

> First-person narrator adds to the sense of credibility. Friendly, cosy tone; not ominous. Prepares us for a remarkable character.

> Capital letters for special places – features of fantasy fiction.

> Building up the mystery.

businesses of his own since they were all small hobbit-boys and hobbit-girls.

All that the unsuspecting Bilbo saw that morning was an old man with a staff. He had a tall pointed blue hat, a long grey cloak, a silver scarf over which his long white beard hung down below his waist, and immense black boots.

> Appearance exotic and intriguing, through use of simple adjectives in a list. Gandalf is not threatening; he is grandfatherly and lovable.

> Bilbo in good mood, in harmony with world around; the simple link word creates contrast with Gandalf.

'Good morning!' said Bilbo, and he meant it. The sun was shining, and the grass was very green. But Gandalf looked at him from long bushy eyebrows that stuck out further than the brim of his shady hat.

'What do you mean?' he said. 'Do you wish me a good morning, or mean that it is a good morning whether I want it or not; or that you feel good this morning; or that it is a morning to be good on?'

> Long speech, use of semi-colons and repetitiveness create Gandalf's impatience and irritation.

From *The Hobbit* by J.R.R. Tolkien

ACTIVITY 25

Look at the paragraph below. It is taken from *Of Mice and Men*. See if you can highlight some of the techniques used by the author to build up a picture of Slim. Make use of the helpful hints contained in the bullet points that follow the passage.

A tall man stood in the doorway. He held a crushed Stetson hat under his arm while he combed his long, black, damp hair straight back. Like the others, he wore blue jeans and a short denim jacket. When he had finished combing his hair he moved into the room, and he moved with a majesty only achieved by royalty and master craftsmen. He was a jerkline skinner, the prince of the ranch, capable of driving ten, sixteen, even twenty mules with a single line to the leaders. He was capable of killing a fly on the wheeler's butt with a bull whip without touching the mule. There was a gravity in his manner and a quiet so profound that all talk stopped when he spoke. His authority was so great that his word was taken on any subject, be it politics or love. This was Slim, the jerkline skinner. His hatchet face was ageless. He might have been thirty-five or fifty. His ear heard more than was said to him, and his slow speech had overtones not of thought, but of understanding beyond thought. His hands, large and lean, were as delicate in their action as those of a temple dancer.

From *Of Mice and Men* by John Steinbeck

> ► At the beginning of his description, how does the writer make Slim appear to be just the same as the other characters?
> ► Is the story being narrated in the first or third person?
> ► Underline significant words or phrases used to describe Slim.
> ► Look for the description of his abilities. How do they further develop the reader's image of the character?
> ► In what other ways is Slim's very positive image created?

ACTIVITY 26

Look at the longer and more difficult passage below and see if you can highlight some of the techniques used by the Nigerian author to build up a picture of the old woman. Again, there are some helpful hints in the bullet points that follow the passage.

The old woman glared at the setting sun. It did not hurt her eyes; for those watering eyeballs had long been shaded by age. She was not leaning on purpose either; she was standing as erect as the weight of years would let her. Her body was wrinkled, her hair long and scraggy, but clean. The river rolled like an angry cloud past her feet, thrashing the opposite shores and, where it descended a precipice further down the course, roaring a war song as if in mockery of her helplessness.

'*Nono,*' meaning 'Great Lady', 'are you all right?'

The old lady turned. A man was standing in the middle of the bridge. . .

'Did you talk to me, young man?' asked the old lady, her voice strong and twenty years younger than the body that gave it source. 'Speak up. I'm half deaf.'

The 'young man' was over forty, towering in height but slightly hunched. His face broke into a smile.

'I said, Great Lady,' he repeated loudly, 'are you all right? Can I help you in any way?'

'*Ekene,*' muttered the old lady, meaning 'Heaven is blest', 'the gods have sent me someone at last.'

'Do you want something done, Great Lady?'

'Yes, son. Could you help me lift this pot to my head?'

The man saw a dotted clay pot standing on the water weeds; it had been filled with water from the spring. 'I came down to the stream when the sun was still high in the sky, level with the top of that tree over there. Now it's almost swallowed up by the heavenly ocean.'

'And you've waited that long?'

'Yes. No one has passed this way since. It must be the farming season. Everyone's on the farm. If I had known the river would be deserted, I would have brought a smaller pitcher to fetch the water, a calabash [a hollowed shell of a gourd/pumpkin used as a water carrier] maybe, so that I wouldn't have to stand here and wait for someone to help me.'

'Don't worry, Great Lady. You won't wait any longer. I am here.'

From *Daughters of the Sun* by Obi Egbuna

▶ Underline significant words or phrases used to describe the old woman.

▶ Is there any evidence to suggest the writer's attitude towards the old lady?

▶ How is she contrasted with the natural world around her and what is the effect of this?

Creating setting and mood

Earlier, we considered how the reader could examine setting. Now we are looking at setting from the other end, analysing what techniques may be used by a writer to develop setting and mood as part of the overall effect of the writing.

A writer will often make a particular effort to engage a reader with the imagined setting of events in a story. In each of the extracts below, think through how the writer has tried to ensure that the reader has a clear picture of the setting. The questions that follow each excerpt are designed to help you with this process of analysis.

ACTIVITY 27

Have a look at the way in which Forrest Carter conjures up the setting in his story *Watch for me on the Mountain*. The story is about a boy and his grandfather who are native American Cherokees and who live in a log cabin in Tennessee.

Me and Granpa clasped our hands behind our heads and watched the moon come up. It was full and yellow, slipping over a far mountain. We could see mighty near a hundred miles, Granpa said, mountains humping and dipping in the moon spray, making shadows and deep purples in their hollows. Fog drifted along in threads, far below us ... moving through the hollows, snaking around the sides of the mountains. One little patch of fog would come around the end of a mountain like a silver boat and bump into another one and they would melt together and take off up a hollow. Granpa said the fog looked alive. Which it did.

From *Watch for me on the Mountain* by Forrest Carter

Think through how the author hopes to bring the setting of this story into your mind's eye.

a How does the writer use colour to create visual images for the reader?

b At the end of the passage Granpa says that 'the fog looked alive'. How has the writer already created the impression of the fog as a living thing?

c The writer is presenting the setting through the eyes of the boy and the grandfather. In what ways does the reader's impression of the setting seem to reflect the relationship between the two characters and their relationship to the landscape?

ACTIVITY 28

Read the extract from the story 'Late Home'. Trevor Millum presents a very different setting through the eyes of a woman who is driving home. She knows that she is going to be late, as she is on a regular basis, and that the person waiting for her at home is going to be both very worried and very angry.

The road narrowed and curved. On either side were high unkempt hedges and behind them the remains of old chalk quarries: large white sores that wouldn't heal. Headlights swept towards her. She kept her hands steady and her eyes rigidly on the air just to the left of the lights. At such times she always felt that she had become invisible to the other driver, who would only realise her existence after the impact. The lorry swept past: a gust of hot air and diesel fumes and total unconcern.

From 'Late Home' by Trevor Millum

a What kind of a picture has the writer created of the setting and the driving conditions the woman is dealing with?

b In what ways does the imagery used by the writer to conjure up the setting also touch on the state of mind of the driver?

ACTIVITY 29

Look now at how Joyce Carol Oates describes her guided tour of a prison.

Next we were taken through the laundry unit which was another cavernous, windowless, fluorescent-glaring space, warm as a slow oven and smelling of damp laundry, disinfectant and oily male sweat. A half-dozen inmates were working, silent, all with sizable stomachs. Except for their sullen faces and their resolutely downcast eyes, these men too gave not the slightest sign of being conscious of their observers. They might have been performers in a long-running play at which we, visiting tourists, were just another audience. The sergeant talked, the inmates went about their work. Folding sheets, towels and uniforms; hauling more laundry out of enormous dryers. Their faces oozed sweat. They moved mechanically, yet with no perceptible beat or rhythm. There could be no pleasure in such work, nor even the angry satisfaction of displeasure. Within minutes the laundry unit became unbearably warm. We visitors were uncomfortable in our winter clothes, our 'professional uniforms'. I wore dark wool, a blazer and a long skirt, and my clothes weighed heavily on me. It was becoming increasingly difficult to concentrate on the sergeant's relentless voice. How mixed up with the glaring fluorescent, that voice of seemingly casual authority. I too had begun to sweat inside my clothes. Like the other visitors I dared not look too closely at inmates who so stonily, with such dignity, refused to look at us. I was thinking 'We didn't put you here! We aren't the ones.'

From *Granta* 63, Autumn 1998, by Joyce Carol Oates

a How does the writer build up a description of conditions in the prison?

b How does the writer include in the description the three groups of people who are present – the prisoners, sergeant and visitors?

c By the end of the description, the reader is aware that the visitor has a very negative view of the prison. How does the writer build up that negative view throughout the passage?

Making use of language

The last piece of the writer's craft jigsaw is one that we have been using and analysing all along – language. Words and phrases have been at the heart of everything we have been studying in the writer's craft.

Why then give it a section of its own? Well, simply to highlight examples of particular uses of language and how you should go about the business of commenting on them.

ACTIVITY 30

This first example is only two sentences long but a skilful choice of language means that this writer has succeeded in conveying to the reader a very negative impression of Skinhead Skinner and his gang.

The notes around the text help to explain the important process regarding **how** this has been achieved.

> Descriptive detail which adds a realistic touch to the unsavoury scene.

> The alliteration combined with the repetition of the word 'skin' in 'Skinhead Skinner' makes him more menacing.

> The choice of the verb 'lurking' reinforces the gang's threatening behaviour.

> Note the use of contrast between the gang's 'mean little eyes' and the innocent 'rosy-cheeked first years'.

That morning Chris Harris almost floated through the rusting iron gates of Greenhall High School. He scarcely noticed Skinhead Skinner and his gang lurking just inside, casting their mean little eyes over the stream of rosy-cheeked first years, selecting with the ease of long-established experts a suitable victim for the day.

> The writer chooses the word 'selecting' as this suggests an element of deliberate malice. The phrase 'with the ease of long-established experts' conveys clearly that they are practised bullies. The description 'suitable victim' successfully reinforces the impression that the first years are being preyed upon by a nasty gang.

From 'The Place of Lions' by Eric Campbell

ACTIVITY 31

Language can be used to create mood or atmosphere.

In the next piece of text the writer is describing what some young people discovered on a night raid to expose the cruelty of puppy farming. The appalling conditions they are confronted with are clearly communicated to the reader.

> The phrase 'lots of little startled eyes' is a striking image, which conveys a sense of the number of puppies in the barn.

> The writer appeals to the reader's sense of smell, which helps to create a realistic scene.

> Short simple sentences are used to give the reader a lot of information in a straightforward way so as to visualise the scene as revealed in Kate's torch beam. The reader sees what Kate sees.

> The reader's sympathetic involvement is further increased with the descriptive details of the vain attempts of the puppies to move and their plaintive cries.

The first thing that struck Elaine was the smell, the warm smell of straw and puppies. Steve raised his torch beam and it lit up lots of little startled eyes. Kate switched on her torch and swung the beam round the barn. There were dogs everywhere. The place was sectioned off into square pens. Each pen held a mother and her litter. The adult dogs were lying on stinking straw and they were tied with just enough room to move their heads to drink and eat from dirty bowls. The puppies moved as the light hit them. Some tried to scramble towards them. Others had no energy to do anything more than add to the chorus of pathetic yelps which filled the barn.

Elaine felt tears well up in her eyes and, quickly, she shook her head in case the others should see. Approaching the nearest pen, she tried to stroke the small fluffy bundles but they crawled away or nipped at her gloved hand.

'Poor little brutes.' Steve's voice was quiet with suppressed anger.

> Emotive language such as 'stinking straw', 'they were tied' and 'dirty bowls' arouses the reader's compassion for the plight of the puppies. These graphic details also make the account more vivid.

> Elaine's response is poignantly and sensitively expressed. Her distress is evident. That the puppies have been so cruelly treated that they cannot accept her affection strikes a genuine chord with the reader.

> Steve's words express his concern for the puppies but the writer also reveals Steve's anger about the conditions in the barn. His reaction to and judgement of the situation are presented in a convincing way and in a manner with which the reader can empathise.

From 'Run with the Hare' by Linda Newbery

ACTIVITY 32

Language can also be used to amuse and entertain the reader. Consider the following extract which is taking a light-hearted view of teenage love.

Michael has been sent into the garden to fetch Fiona, the daughter of his father's friend, for her lunch. She is lying in the garden hammock. They have never met before and Michael is immediately smitten.

The writer contrasts their reactions to each other in an amusing way. The reference to 'the garden wheelbarrow' is original and very witty.

The use of first-person narrative involves the reader. The short, blunt opening sentence successfully conveys Michael's pleasant surprise.

I stopped in my tracks. 'Uh, hello. I'm Mike. I expect they told you I exist.'

She looked up with the same breathless interest she would have shown in the garden wheelbarrow. 'Oh, yes.' It wasn't much but it was a beginning.

'Michael,' my mother called from the french windows. 'I need some help, dear. We're all having lunch in the garden.'

The list of adjectives conveys Michael's elation as well as a sense of his pleasantly bubbly personality. The reader's interest in the narrative is agreeably sustained.

We have no domestic help. On the other hand we have a washing-up machine, called Michael, and a chair-carrying and table-laying machine also called Michael. From one point of view it was a nuisance that these two were staying for lunch, because it meant work for me, but from every other point of view it was smashing, brilliant, fabulous, knock-out.

Note how effective the repetition is in adding to the reader's enjoyment.

'Oh, dear,' said the girl, trying to sit up in the hammock. 'I didn't know we were staying for lunch. I'd better go in and wash.'

The choice of the verb 'wheezed' is most apt as it amusingly describes how he speaks.

His reaction to her touch is deliberately exaggerated. This use of hyperbole injects liveliness and creates a hilariously ridiculous image.

'It's hard to get out of that thing. I'll help you,' I wheezed and I moved forward and held the sides of the hammock to steady it. She put one hand on my shoulder as she lightly jumped down and the electric thrill went right down to the soles of my feet. When I moved I expected to see scorch marks on the grass the shape and size of my foot soles.

Was I in love with her? Yes, I was already asking myself that, though our acquaintance could hardly be said to have ripened yet.

Comical internal dialogue is another clever device to entertain the reader.

'I'll show you where the bathroom is,' I said, frisking around on my invisible paws and wagging my invisible tail.

'I know already,' she said. She laughed, musically. Her laugh sounded like condensed milk being poured over a xylophone. I liked it.

The writer employs a metaphor to compare Michael's behaviour to that of an over-enthusiastic puppy dog.

This simile is a memorably imaginative way to describe Fiona's laugh.

The short concluding sentence contrasts with the one before it, adding variety and interest.

From 'You Can't Keep Out the Darkness' by John Wain

ACTIVITY 33

Dialogue plays a vital role in engaging and sustaining the reader's interest in a story. Conversations reveal much about characters and can, for example, inject humour or demonstrate a sense of hostility between two people.

You're going to consider two different extracts from a story about a girl who, despite knowing her mother will strongly disapprove, goes ahead and has her ears pierced. The first piece, the beginning of the story, captures the reader's attention because it is entertaining to read. Let's examine how dialogue, along with other aspects of language usage, combine to create an effective and enjoyable piece of writing.

> This witty simile adds a humorous touch. It is also an economic way to indicate Karen's extrovert personality and the contrast between the two friends.

> Karen's amusingly OTT description of how ears are pierced gives the story a lively opening.

> Be alert to when writers reveal their characters' thoughts. Internal monologue is often used as a humorous device. Mandy's obvious discomfort about having her ears pierced is being dealt with light-heartedly.

'It's all right, Mandy, honest, you don't feel a thing. They just stick an ice cube behind your ear, get a darning needle and a mallet and then, wallop, it's done.' Mandy looked less than reassured; not that she took Karen seriously; her ears looked like a graveyard for redundant curtain rings so it couldn't hurt that much.

The shop assistant took them through to a stuffy room at the back. Mandy wondered how clean it was. 'Choose what studs you fancy,' the girl said, handing her a display card. 'I'll go wash my hands and get the gun.'

'Will she be doing it?' Mandy asked.

> Descriptive details poke gentle fun at Mandy's predicament. Note the entertaining reference to the piercing gun as 'a contraption that looked as though it might need a licence'.

'Who'd you expect?' said Karen. 'A doctor? Come on Mand, choose. . .these hearts are nice.'

The girl returned with a battered case from which she took a plastic bottle half-full of clear liquid and a metallic contraption that looked as though it might need a licence.

'I'd like some of these, please,' Mandy said, indicating a pair of plain studs, and the girl slotted one into her gun. She up-ended the plastic bottle on a pink cotton-wool ball and dabbed at Mandy's ear lobes. 'Anaesthetic?' she queried hopefully.

> This interchange is made amusing by the contrast between Mandy's anxious tone and Karen's sarcastic remark about a doctor. Her dismissal of her friend's fears is delivered in a chirpy manner without malice so the reader enjoys the joke at Mandy's expense.

'No. . .antiseptic,' the girl replied. 'Don't bother to freeze yer ears now. It's so quick see. Not time for it to hurt. . . Hold still.'

> The play on words between 'anaesthetic' and 'antiseptic' adds more humour. The use of short sentences and onomatopoeia help create an amusing scene as the reader can empathise with how Mandy must be reacting.

Zap! The thin metal shaft shot into her ear. And then the other one. Zap!

'Now, don't take them out for six weeks.' the girl impressed on her. 'Just dab 'em with the lotion and give 'em a daily twiddle. . .like yer was winding yer watch up. . . And don't wear heavy rings for four months else yer might split yer lobes.' Mandy shuddered. 'OK?' asked the girl.

> The colloquial speech adds realism and energy. The gruesome details are funny as is the girl's question to Mandy.

Now you have a go at analysing the following piece of dialogue. This conversation takes place later in the story when Mandy returns home to face her mother.

The writer makes the inevitable confrontation very convincing. How does the dialogue help to convey the tension between Mandy and her mother? In what other ways does the writer use language to create this strained atmosphere?

Some words and phrases you should pay particular attention to are highlighted in red for you.

'Where've you been, Amanda? You're late. I was worried.' Her mother lifted her head from her book. She noticed immediately.

'Take those out, Amanda.'

'But mother. . .'

'Take them out. . .you know precisely what I think about ear-piercing. Take them out. Take them out or I'll take them out for you.'

Her mother moved towards her. Mandy imagined her hand reaching up, ripping out the studs. She felt faint with rage and fear and frustration. She took out the earrings and clasped them tightly behind her back.

'Give them to me.'

'Please let me keep them.'

'How can I possibly let you keep them? You obviously can't be trusted not to wear them. Give them to me.'

She loathed her mother at that moment. She handed over the studs, her eyes spiked with tears, and watched immobile as her mother took them away. She knew then they'd gone, gone for good.

Both extracts from 'Statements of Account' by Jenny Hursell

ACTIVITY 34

In this extract the writer is describing what happens when a young man called John attempts to climb an old factory chimney.

The tension mounts as John realises his mistake in attempting this stunt. How has the writer used words and phrases to communicate a sense of John's fear?

As with the previous extract, language you should pay particular attention to is highlighted in red to help you.

John's gaze travelled slowly to the top of the chimney but he didn't move or speak. Taking a deep breath he purposefully gripped the side of the ladder, climbed some rungs rapidly and then with slow caution ascended another four. His toe dislodged a piece of mortar and he heard it clink against the ladder on its way to the ground. He paused, frightened. Above him he saw the ladder converge at the top like railway lines. He had a long way to go yet, and on looking down to measure his distance from the ground he saw, in one swaying moment, the old drying sheds buckle and stretch like an accordion.

He clutched grimly to the ladder and allowed his head to clear. Sweat oozed in blobs on his forehead and his hands became clammy. In front of him he saw tiny hairs of moss growing like moles between the bricks and he noticed with rising terror that some of the bricks were cracked. He closed his eyes, swallowed with difficulty, and made an attempt to descend. His foot missed the lower rung and his trouser-leg caught on it and rolled back, and for a moment he felt free air on his bare leg. He drew his two feet together, twined his arms round a rung of the ladder and remained there – frozen in fright.

A tizzling sound trembled through the sides of the ladder. His workmates were hammering on it, signalling to him to come down. He was terrified to move or to look up or look down. He heard Tim call up to him, but what advice was given he couldn't make out. He clung to the rung above his head and closed his eyes to shut out the drunken tilting of the chimney.

From 'Steeplejacks' by Michael McLaverty

ACTIVITY 35

Now it's time to put into practice all you have learned in this section about how writers use language.

Below is a lengthy extract from the beginning of quite a scary story. Answer the following question.

How has the writer built up a growing sense of unease in this piece of writing? Consider how words and phrases are used to describe:

▸ the house and its surroundings
▸ Connie's thoughts and reactions
▸ how events unfold.

Connie began to have the feeling of dread and uneasiness in the taxi but told herself it was not reasonable. She thrust away the feeling as the taxi rolled out across the neck of land beyond most of the houses. The red, dying sun cast long shadows across the road.

The taxi stopped and the last thin sliver of crimson sun went down below the world's edge. Dusk was already here. But everything looked perfectly normal. The house looked neat and hospitable, and it was good to be back. She paid the taxi driver and he obligingly put her suitcases inside the door. The uneasy feeling intensified as he left. But she tried not to heed it.

It continued while she heard the taxi moving away and purring down the road. But it remained essentially the same – a sort of formless restlessness and apprehension – until she went into the kitchen. Then the feeling changed.

She was in the kitchen, with the close smell of a shut-up house about her, when she noticed the change. Her suitcases still lay in the hall where the taxi driver had piled them. The front door was still open to let in fresh air. And quite suddenly she had an urgent certainty that there was something here that she should notice. But, surely, this sensation was just as absurd as the feeling she'd had in the taxi.

There was a great silence outside the house. This was dusk, and the bird and insect noises were growing fainter. There were no neighbours near to make other sounds.

She turned on the refrigerator and it began to make a companionable humming sound. She turned on the water and it gushed. But now her anxiety took a new form. It seemed that every movement produced a noise which advertised her presence, and she felt that was some reason to be utterly still. And that really was nonsense too.

She glanced around the kitchen. Afterwards she remembered that she had looked straight at the back door without seeing what there was to be seen. She went firmly down the hall. Then she went out of doors to look at her flowers.

The garden looked only a little neglected. The west was a fading, already dim glory of red and gold. She smelled the comfortable, weary smells of the late summer evening, which would presently give way to the sharper, fresher scents of night. There was the tiny darting shadow of a bat overhead, black against the dark sapphire sky. It was the time when, for a little space, peace seems to enfold all the world. But the nagging uneasiness persisted even out here.

There was a movement by the garage, but it failed to catch her eye. If she had looked – even if she failed to see the movement – she might have seen the motorcycle. It did not belong here, but it was leaning against the garage wall as if its owner had ridden it here and leaned it confidentially where it would be hidden from anyone looking across the bay. But Connie noticed nothing. She simply felt uneasy.

She found herself going nervously back towards the house. The sunset colours faded, and presently all would be darkness outside. She heard her footsteps on the gravelled walk. Occasional dry leaves brushed against her feet. It seemed to her that she hurried, which was ridiculous. So she forced herself to walk naturally and resisted an impulse to look about.

That is why she failed to notice the pantry window.

She came to the front of the house. Her heels made clicking sounds on the steps. She felt a need to be very quiet, to hide herself.

Yet she had no reason for fear in anything she actually had noticed. She hadn't seen anything odd about the back door or the pantry window, and she hadn't noticed the motorcycle or the movement by the garage. The logical explanation for her feeling of terror was simply that it was dark and she was alone.

She repeated that explanation as she forced herself to enter the dark front doorway.

She wanted to gasp with relief as she felt for the switch and the lights came on. The dark rooms remaining were more terrifying then than the night outside. So she went all over the ground floor, turning on lights, and tried not to think of going upstairs. There was no one within call and no one but the taxi driver even knew she was here. Anything could happen.

In the lighted living room she had the feeling of someone staring at her from the dark outside. It was unbearable.

'Ridiculous!' Connie told herself.

She got a suitcase and started for the stairs. It was deep night now. If she looked out – say at the garage – she would see nothing. Somewhere there was dismal cooing. Doves.

She climbed the stairs into darkness. Nothing happened. She pressed a switch and the passage sprang into light. She breathed again. She went into her bedroom. There was dust on the dressing table.

Then she saw cigarette ends on the rug. Scorched places. Someone had sat here in this bedroom, smoking and carelessly dropping cigarette ends on the rug and crushing them out.

Connie stood with every muscle in her body turned to stone.

From 'Uneasy Homecoming' by Will Jenkins

Answering effectively

The most common mistake that candidates make with this third question, is to continue answering in the same style as that used for the first two questions. You will not score highly by telling the examiner what the writer has done – this question is about **how** it has been done.

In the examples below, the students were asked to consider how the writer sustains the interest of the reader. One of the examiner's bullet points referred to the way the story finishes. The first example shows how not to answer.

> ✗ *The story has a very exciting ending. It is only when they cross the line that we know that Peter has been successful.*

This candidate has fallen into the trap of saying what the writer has done and doing some storytelling as well. In the next example the student addresses the question – how the ending helps to sustain interest.

> ✓ *The writer has developed a highly dramatic situation that is only resolved in the final paragraph. By doing this, the writer has ensured that the reader is kept in suspense until the very end of the story.*

The other major difficulty for candidates is an alarming inability to make full use of the bullet points provided by the examiner. These bullet points are there to give you direction – effectively the examiner is saying, 'Write about these.' They can valuably be used to guide your groundwork on the text as well as giving you the subheadings needed for a relevant answer.

6 Time to get practical

In this section of the book, you have learnt the skills required in answering the three different types of question that appear in CCEA's GCSE English, Paper 1 Section A. Now it is important that you practise these skills, on a complete passage and preferably under examination conditions. In the actual examination, you will only have **one hour** for this section of the Paper.

Below is a series of key points to use as a revision checklist.

▸ Make sure that you follow the instructions given on the examination paper. The examiner has tried to help you **organise** your response, especially with regard to use of time.

▸ 'Spend about **15 minutes reading** the passage carefully.' This means not only studying the story carefully and methodically but also:

- underlining or highlighting key parts (for example, interesting words and phrases); and
- making brief notes in the margin of the paper (for example, comments that occur to you about a character).

▸ Make **effective** use of your time.

- Do not overrun the time suggested for each answer. Note that the examiner has guided you as to how long to spend on each answer.
- Especially, leave yourself enough time to answer the last question fully. This question usually carries more marks than the first two. You must get it finished!
- In each answer, go into detail and make as many relevant points as you can in the time suggested. It is important that you do not finish the exam early!

▸ When answering individual questions remember to use the skills of **skim-reading**. Look quickly again at the relevant part of the passage and identify clearly the material that will help you write an appropriate answer. For example:

 ● if the question says – 'What do you learn about Bill? Use evidence from lines 1–50 to support your answer', then you should refer to this part of the passage again, identifying in it all that is suggested about Bill.

▸ Remember that in your study of the passage you are expected not only to recognise explicit facts but also to spot implicit meaning that is **hinted at**. Note the facts but also read 'between the lines'!

▸ Finally, the examiner always tries to select a passage that will interest you or with which you can empathise. It is important to remember that if you can **enjoy** the story presented in the passage and really **engage with** the situation and the characters, you are more likely to write interesting answers, which will earn good marks from the examiner. Dull answers do not impress!

The two test pieces that follow are typical of Paper 1 Section A.

FOUNDATION TIER SAMPLE PAPER

Paper 1   Section A

This section tests **reading** skills.

- Spend about **15 minutes reading** the passage carefully.

- Answer **all three** questions.

(This story is set in the 1970s and is about a teenage girl who goes to a formal dance for the first time.)

As soon as Michael asked her to go to the rugby club formal, Lynn knew her mother was the one she had to convince. 'You want to go to a formal dance? And you're only seventeen? Well I don't know about that. What does your father say?'

Her father said, 'She has to get used to the ways of the world sooner or later.'

'Let it be later then,' replied her mother. 'The ways of the world are soon enough got used   5
to when she's left school.'

From then on, it was a matter of being careful in her answers to a multitude of questions. Who was he anyway? Did she know his people? No, so he could be anybody. What age was he? Eighteen! They'd no sense at eighteen. And did he smoke and did she go into pubs with him?   10

'Look, mummy,' she said patiently, 'he drinks very little – he has to play rugby. Sure, you don't make a fuss about me going to the disco, where some stupid kids are full to the eyeballs.'

'But there you're with girlfriends, not dancing with one boy all night. Dancing with one person all night long is too serious at your age.'   15

But Lynn swung things her way in the end. It helped when she admitted she wasn't all that keen on Michael anyway, it was more the occasion she was going for.

On the night of the formal, Michael called for her, shook hands with her parents and promised to have her back on the dot of one-thirty. Her long dress rustled as she walked down the path and when she paused at the door of his car to gather the folds and slip into   20
the front seat it was like a movement rehearsed a thousand times. Her mother, watching from behind the living-room curtain, said, 'Isn't she very young?'

'It'll broaden her horizons,' her father replied. 'That's only the front path out there, not the aisle.'

★ ★ ★

The house that night seemed empty without Lynn. Her elder brother Gordon came in at   25
twelve and wondered out loud how Cinderella was getting on.

'Give over!' snapped his mother. 'And don't torture her tomorrow with your banter, you hear.'

They didn't wait up for her, but her mother couldn't sleep for worrying. She couldn't understand how her husband could snore so contentedly with his only daughter out till all   30
hours, 'broadening her horizons' as he put it.

The luminous green figures on the bedside clock said one-forty. They were late! Time meant nothing to young ones nowadays. At two-fifteen she was about to wake her husband, when she heard the key in the lock. She was quickly out of bed and at the head of the stairs.   35

'Are you there, Lynn?'

'Yes, Mummy, Michael's just going. I'll be up in a minute or two.'

'Put the chain on the door then, dear.'

★ ★ ★

Back in bed, she finally dozed off as she heard Michael's car leaving the street.

Lynn woke late the next morning and lay for a long time, savouring the activities of the night before. She'd hardly been off the dance-floor the whole time, except during the meal. Getting through all those courses had been like a day's work. At twelve-thirty she skipped down the stairs to the phone.   40

'Is that you, Lynn?' she heard her mother shout. 'Lunch!'

'In a minute, Mummy. I'm just phoning my friend Gillian.'   45

'Well, Gillian, I went! Yes, with Michael. No, he's OK, but I'd rather you-know-who had asked me. Still, maybe another time. You should have seen all the class people there. And the atmosphere! Food was lovely, lamb cutlets. The tableware was out of this world. My people are so ordinary. Gillian, it was like another way of life, sitting there cutting up all kinds of everything with a hundred different knives and forks. I had to show Michael which to use first. Honestly, men know nothing. Yes. Uh-huh. I will. I'll come round later. Bye.'   50

Her mother smiled as she sat down at the kitchen table, asked if she'd had a nice time but didn't press for details. A loaf spilled in slices out of its wrapper and at each of the four places the lettuce leaves of a humble salad flounced over the edge of a plate, touching the soiled cloth. The battered teapot, favoured for its easy pour, squatted in its accustomed place at the centre of the table. It was all so throughother.   55

'How's the boyfriend, then?' Her ridiculous brother started his nonsense right away. Lynn knew better than to get angry. That was always the object of his game.

'Mummy, have you a clean spoon for the sugar? This one's all gooey.'   60

'Fussy, aren't we?' Gordon chipped in.

In actual fact there was a lot to be fussy about. She noticed the way her father chewed with his mouth open, the dark flecks of burned toast in the butter, the thick gunge round the cap of the sauce bottle.

'Just a cup of tea for me, please,' Lynn said. 'I'm not that hungry.'   65

After lunch she said to her parents, 'Actually, I'd like to discuss something with you.' There was a considerable silence, then a suspicious 'Oh?' from her mother.

'Speak up, love,' said her father. 'We always listen.'

'Well, it's just that I don't like the way we. . .the way we sometimes eat.'

Her mother lifted some dishes from the table and dumped them noisily in the sink. Her father looked at her grimly.   70

'Mother, she doesn't like the way we eat.'

'So I hear. Ask her what's wrong with it.'

'What's wrong with what we eat?'

'It's very hard to put into words.'   75

'Try,' said her father dryly. 'I'm sure you'll manage.'

'It's not *what* we eat, it's *how*. It's got. . .no *atmosphere,* if you see what I mean.'

'Mother, our eating has no atmosphere in it,' her father echoed, as Lynn blushed.

'I don't mean we should have lamb cutlets and fancy cheeses all the time. It's *how* we eat – it's so. . .*plain.*'   80

Lynn's mother angrily faced her daughter. 'Anything else you don't like about us?' she asked. 'Maybe we should change the way we talk, too?'

'No!' Lynn said, alarmed by how big the issue had become in the space of a few sentences. 'That's not fair. I didn't mean it like that.'

'It sounds fair to me,' her father said. 'I think you've got a bloody nerve!'   85

Fighting back tears of frustration at her parents' misunderstanding, Lynn rushed out. The mother looked daggers at the father. 'So much for broad horizons!' she said.

★ ★ ★

Later, at the tea-time meal, Gordon was totally bewildered by what went on. His mother wore her necklace of imitation pearls as she loudly uncorked a bottle of red wine and delivered a slurp into each of four cut-crystal glasses. His father, wearing the overalls he'd   90 been painting in, spread a linen napkin over his knee and spent a long time tasting the wine: 'Dark and slightly nutty. Delicious. Takes a decent red for steak, doesn't it, Lynn?'

Gordon was amazed that his sister had nothing to say, for there was a talking point everywhere. The silver candlesticks, for a start! He fiddled with the heavy, pearl-   95 handled knives lying by his plate. Every piece of cutlery on the glittering table matched its fellow.

'Oh, lah-de-dah!' Gordon said. 'Are we expecting royalty?' Glancing at Lynn, he saw her sitting with her head down. He asked, 'Is it this knife here to start with?'   100

'You start at the outside and work in, as you know rightly,' his mother said.

'One day, my lad,' said his father, 'you may need to know these things, when we all become toffs. We don't want to be disgraced, do we, Lynn?   105

'Yes, that's right,' Lynn said, bitterly.

After tea, Lynn washed the dishes while her parents watched telly. It took a full hour, for every dish in the house had been used in the preparation of the six-course meal. Every knife, fork and spoon had to be thoroughly dried and slotted back into a special box with a satin finish inside.   110

Later, Lynn went to bed early and read. On his way to bed, Gordon timidly knocked on her door and came in.

'What's been going on?' he asked, still puzzled. 'You were all OK when I left at lunch. Then I arrive back to the Mad Hatter's tea party. You know what they're at now? Curled up on the settee, drinking red wine and watching Dracula!'   115

'I criticised their eating habits,' Lynn explained. 'I only said everything was a bit plain. This is their revenge.'

'So that's why they did all that?' Gordon replied. 'Need their heads examined!'

On his way out, Gordon flicked off her light, just to annoy her.

'Switch it back on!' Lynn snapped at him.   120

'Switch it on yourself, snob,' he chuckled as he left, dodging the heavy paperback she threw after him.

From 'Aristocrockery' by Sam McBratney

1 Spend about **12 minutes** on this question. Use **evidence from the whole passage** as a basis for your answer.

Imagine you are Lynn's mother. Write a diary entry in which you present your thoughts and feelings about your daughter's recent behaviour.

Present your thoughts about:

- Lynn going to the formal dance
- her attempt to influence family eating habits
- anything else you think is relevant.

[9 marks]

2 Spend about **12 minutes** on this question. Use **evidence from lines 54–65 and 88–97** to support your answer.

The writer describes the family's lunch and then their evening meal. How does the writer develop the reader's picture of these two very different meals?

[9 marks]

3 Spend about **20 minutes** on this question. Use **evidence from the whole passage** to support your answer.

This passage presents a lively account of a typical family conflict. How does the writer try to make his story interesting?

Write about:

- the relationships between the characters
- the humour in the situation
- the use of words and phrases.

[12 marks]

HIGHER TIER SAMPLE PAPER

Paper 1   Section A

This section tests **reading** skills.

- Spend about **15 minutes reading** the passage carefully.

- Answer **all three** questions.

___

(The story is mainly told from Samuel's point of view.)

His father sat with his legs stretched out into the hearth, his stockinged feet so close to the
crackling furnace of the fire that steam rose in steady wisps. He sat in his armchair at the
side of the chimney where only a stranger, ignorant of its private ownership, would dare to
sit. As he watched his father dozing, his head jerking at intervals on to his chest, he
noticed how soiled and threadbare the headrest had become, worn almost shiny with use,   5
and the white circles on its wooden arms where for twenty years his father had rested his
mug. While all the meals were taken at the white-clothed table, his father always moved to
the armchair for his tea. It did not matter whether there was company or not, he never
broke his habit, and while select visitors might take their tea out of the best rose-
patterned tea-set, he would insist on his bucket of a mug.   10

As he dozed now, his head lolling to one side, the fire lit up the weathered tautness of his
face and the tracery of tiredness circling his eyes, and even in this fitful drowse, it was as
if his body was struggling to fight off some deeper sleep.

In the kitchen he could hear his mother setting the washed dishes back in the cupboard
and the tinkle of cutlery dropping into the drawer. His father's breathing grew heavier. In   15
a short while, however, he would wake up and shuffle off to find some work to do, as if
guilty about the time he had wasted. He was a man whose whole life was founded on work.
Away from the farm he was like a little boy lost in a foreign and unfriendly city, where
nothing was familiar and nothing had purpose. There was, too, a deep vein of arrogance in
him which produced an unshakeable conviction that no one was able to do things as well   20
as he could. Certainly not his son. He had also, just below the surface, a temper which
could blow sudden and fierce, and which as a child he had often experienced, usually
for the crime of 'answering back'. His father grunted in his sleep and his mouth
opened slightly.

His mother came in with her sewing box under her arm, sat down and then began to mend   25
a ripped knee in a pair of blue overalls.

His father grunted again. They both glanced at him, then smiled at each other,
momentarily linked in a little conspiracy of friendship which excluded the sleeping man.
She returned to her sewing, forming close, delicate stitches. Doing a job well was a matter
of honour – in that, his parents were well matched.   30

He watched her as she sat with her head bent over the sewing. It unsettled him to see how
old she was beginning to look. It had hit him first on his return from his second year at
university. Like most sons who loved their mother, he had assumed that she would go on
forever, unchanging and untouched by time or illness. As he looked at her now, he saw a

woman whose hair was whitening like a frosted hedgerow, and whose hand shook when 35
she tried to thread a needle. There was still an inner wick of strength, but it no longer
burned so brightly or seemed so invincible.

His father started to wake up, and rubbed his mouth with the back of his hand. Suddenly,
the dog started to bark loudly in the kitchen. His mother paused in her sewing and said,
'He's here! Quiet, boy, quiet!' His father jumped up and grabbed his boots, and without 40
opening them, forced his feet down into them, stamping on the floor to get them on, as if
crushing some poisonous insect. He followed his father into the kitchen.

Ordering the dog to stay, his father opened the door only wide enough to allow both of
them to edge through. They slipped into the yard. The cold night air stung their faces and
a cutting wind stabbed at their clothes. A bright, whole moon cast a milky light over the 45
yard and sharp-iced stars trembled nervously. They walked slowly towards the barn, their
eyes scanning every shadow for any flicker of movement, and their ears straining for the
slightest rustle, but a silent stillness held everywhere, calm and undisturbed. As a cloud
scudded across the moon, they paused and stared into the pools of darkness which formed
at the base of the barn and round the sheds and outhouses beyond it. Glancing at each 50
other, they shook their heads as if to say they saw nothing, then his father nodded in the
direction of the hen-run. They checked the hen-run and looked around but could find no
trace of an attempted incursion.

'Come on – there's no point freezing to death out here. It'll not come back the night, but
we'll let the dog out to run round for an hour or so just to be sure.' 55

'Are you certain it was here?'

His father looked at him as if he had just asked a foolish question.

'It was here, all right. The dog knew and as soon as I set foot in the yard I knew too. But
I'll get him in the end. Sooner or later, he'll make a mistake, then I'll burn his tail.'

They turned back to the farmhouse, walking in silence. He thought about the fox. He 60
wondered where it was at that exact moment – perhaps slinking through some sheltering
hedgerow, or looking down at the yellow-eyed farmhouse from the dark safety of the
woods. He harboured no romantic fancies about it and would kill it too if he got the chance.
Anyone who had seen the hen-coop that morning last August after the fox had broken in
couldn't help but feel the same way. For his father, that was the beginning of something 65
which started as a desire to protect his property and livelihood, but gradually turned into
an intensely personal battle where wits were pitted against each other, until it became
almost a struggle for supremacy over the land itself.

In the morning there was a light skim of snow brushing the ground and icicles hanging
from the guttering of the house. He had offered his father a morning's work – he needed 70
the rest of the day to work on an essay due at the start of the new term.

'Well, let's get at it, then. If you're on a half-day, I'd better get the most out of you.'

'Studying is hard work too,' he said defensively as he followed his father into the yard to
chop logs. They carried out the trunk of a tree they had felled the previous summer, and
using a cross-cut saw, began to divide it into workable sections. He could feel his father's 75
strength as his shoulder pushed the saw towards him through the wood and he tried to
match it as he pushed it back. The blade cut straight and deep, and as snow began to fall
lightly, the push and pull bedded itself into a steady rhythm. Then gradually, almost

imperceptibly, he sensed that his father's push towards him was weakening. He glanced up at his face and saw it tight and pained. Flakes of snow had whitened his hair. He suddenly looked old. His father was holding on grimly to the saw, determined to see the job finished. As his father pushed the saw once more towards him, he held it tightly and did not push it back. His father pulled, then looked up at him with confused watery eyes. 80

'We've done enough, Da. We'll go inside now,' he said, his voice stronger and surer than he really felt. 85

His father said nothing, but straightened himself up. Leaving the saw embedded in the wood, he took his father by the arm, and, shoulder to shoulder, they walked slowly towards the house. His mother seemed to know what had happened. They helped him into his chair and she knelt at his feet and gently removed his boots.

'No need for fussing, now. It's just a wee tightness. In a few minutes I'll be as right as rain,' his father reassured her. 90

'You're stopping there the rest of the day,' ordered his mother in a voice which brooked no argument.

He went back out to the yard and cleaned the saw. When he returned his father was sleeping, watched over by his mother as she did the ironing. 95

'How long's this been going on?' he asked, conscious that things had been kept from him.

'We decided there wasn't any point worrying you with something you couldn't do anything about. It's his heart, but everything could be all right if he doesn't overdo things. And you've enough on your mind with your studies.'

'But I could have come home more weekends than I did, and helped out more.' 100

'It's not the weekends he needs help – it's the five days in between.' She readjusted the shirt almost angrily. She continued ironing and as she smoothed invisible creases and wrinkles he knew that she was working up to saying something – something important. She hesitated, then set the iron on its heel, rubbing her hand along the ironing board.

'Your father – well, both of us – have always hoped that after you got your education you'd come back and run the farm with him. In a few years, maybe, take it over. He's a proud man, and he'll never ask, but it's what he's always wanted. One thing's for sure – if he goes on like this he'll kill himself' 105

There were tears in her eyes, and she tried to hide them by snatching a towel out of the basket and shooting the iron up and down it.

'I've never asked you for anything before, Samuel, but I'm asking you now. Asking you just to think about it.' 110

'My heart's never been in farming, Ma – you know that. I've never wanted to make it the rest of my life. I've always done my share, but it's not even as if we get on well together.'

'Your father's not a man who shows his feelings, and I know he hasn't always been easy on you, but I know, deep down, he's proud of you. When you got to university there wasn't a body on the road he didn't tell.' 115

'He'd never be able to sit back and hand the running of the farm over to me. You know he'd –'

His mother motioned him to be quiet. His father was stirring in the chair. 'All I'm asking you to do is think about it. That's all,' she said softly. 120

'Boys-a-dear, I must've dropped off,' his father said. 'Is it still snowing outside?'

'It is, and you'll not be stirring over the door,' asserted his mother.

'Will you stop fussing, woman. I'm as right as rain.'   125

But for the rest of the afternoon, he pottered aimlessly about the house. After tea, his talk turned again to the fox.

'Thon same boy'll be back the night. I feel it. I think we'll have a wee surprise waiting for him. I'm going to set the trap.'

His father must have caught the look on both their faces, because he tried to reassure   130
them. 'There's no need to worry. I'll be careful with it.'

Later that evening, his father brought the trap down from the high shelf of the barn. He carried it out into the snow-blanched night, and after making sure dog and cats were safely locked up, set it close to the hen-run, baiting it with the remains of the chicken which had made the lunchtime soup.   135

He told his parents he was going to have an early night. When, eventually, he fell asleep, his restless dreams were a web of fragmentary images in which he found himself lost in a tangle of tall hedgerows, whose thorns reached out to scratch his arms. As he struggled to escape he could feel the burning yellow eyes of the fox following and watching him through the chinks in the hedge. In his dream, he knew that somewhere sitting waiting was the   140
cruel trap, its perfect teeth glinting in the moonlight.

In the morning his father rustled with impatience to inspect the trap. As he followed his father round the sheds to the hen-run, he felt suddenly frightened by what they might find.

The trap was closed – he could see it in the distance. He felt an inexplicable surge of relief.   145
There was no fox in it. But, as they drew closer, they saw dark splashes of blood spotting the snow. His father ran and, kneeling over the trap, cleared away the snow with his hands, like a child digging in sand. Then, with frightened eyes, he stood aside to show him the fox's paw his hands had uncovered.

'He's eaten through his own paw to escape. He's gnawed his own paw right off. I've heard   150
of it, but I'd never have believed it, only I'm looking at it with my own eyes,' his father said, his voice quiet but his hands shaking. 'Go and get the gun and the dog. We'll follow the trail back up to its den. We've got him now.'

'I'll take no part in this,' he said, his voice cutting high and clear through the cold air. 'I'll have no hand in its killing.'   155

His father stood up, his eyes red and raw, his fists clenched by his sides as if he were going to strike him. Words started on his lips but melted away into nothingness. Suddenly, he turned and, without speaking, headed back the way he'd come. For a second he watched his father's heavy trudge across the snow as black shadows of crows circled overhead, and the birch trees shivered on the skyline. He looked at the trap again. Then he turned and   160
followed his father, leaving his own prints in the snow.

From 'The Trap' by David Park

1 Spend about **12 minutes** on this question. Use **evidence from the whole passage** to support your answer.

What sort of person is Samuel's father?

[9 marks]

2 Spend about **12 minutes** on this question. Use **evidence from lines 43–53** to answer this question.

How does the writer use the setting to build up the tension at this point in the story?

[9 marks]

3 Spend about **20 minutes** on this question. Use **evidence from the whole passage** to support your answer.

How has the writer created a story that is interesting to read?

In your answer you should refer to:

• how the story builds up to the shock ending

• the use of descriptive language

• the use of dialogue.

[12 marks]

PAPER 1
SECTION B
Writing to review, analyse and comment

THE ASSESSMENT OBJECTIVES

These are the skills and abilities that this **writing** section tests.

Students are expected to show the ability to:

The percentage of the marks given to the different assessment objectives

66.66%

a put across what has to be said in a clear and original way

b take note of the purpose and the target audience, and use a writing form that suits both

c organise ideas into sentences and paragraphs

d make use of language and structure techniques to create the desired effect

e present work clearly and neatly

33.33%

f use a range of sentence structures effectively

g punctuate accurately

h spell accurately.

1 What's required?

You will be given a question or statement (for example, 'Why should we give to charities?') and along with it you will be given about four related points. These will offer a range of views and stances on the subject.

How will I go about answering?

a   You will be expected to **review** the points given, plus present some more of your own. These you will **analyse** as well as including your own ideas and anecdotes. You will be expected to **comment** on all of them.

b   You can approach the question in one of three ways: you can present a case in favour of the statement given, take the opposing view or adopt a neutral stance. No matter which of these approaches you choose, it is important that you **consider all sides of the issue**. A good answer to this question will have presented a rounded view of the topic.

c   Remember that the examiner is the audience for this piece of writing so adopt a style and range of words and phrases that is suitable for this audience.

d   Organise the material so that your essay develops in an ordered and structured manner. Remember to express yourself fluently and accurately.

---

2 Planning

There are a number of steps you should work through when writing your essay; the first of these is planning.

It is absolutely essential that you plan your essay before beginning to write. Your plan is the foundation of your essay. If you plan before you write it means that your answer will be relevant, your ideas will be clearly organised and you will not run out of things to write.

Before you begin the process of planning, you should look carefully at the points given in the exam paper. These will direct you towards some of the major issues related to the topic as well as highlighting different views about it.

Planning is normally quite a messy business because at this early stage the first thing to do is to have a brainstorming session. The aim of this is to get all of the ideas in your head down on paper quickly. Do not worry about organising them – this will come later.

ACTIVITY 1

Below is a range of points given to help students respond to the statement, **'Watching television is bad for you'**. Sort them into points that could be used to support this statement and points that could be used to argue against it.

▸ Watching television kills conversation.

▸ A range of educational programmes is shown.

▸ Television provides instant access to news and other information.

▸ Television discourages play amongst young people.

▸ Television advertising puts unfair pressure on consumers.

▸ Television programmes are entertaining.

You will then need to come up with some points of your own, so brainstorm your ideas on the topic. You are looking for any other relevant points either for or against this statement. When you are brainstorming your ideas you might find it helpful to divide your page into points for and against.

POINTS FOR	**POINTS AGAINST**

Alternatively you might decide to plan your essay using a spider diagram.

Points for   **Points against**

Watching television
is bad for you

3 Analysis

At this stage you should have a list of points for and against the given statement.

Now it is time to examine these points in depth. This is known as **analysis**. The best way to analyse the points given, as well as your own, is to question or challenge them. This process might enable you to make up your mind about your opinion on the issue. Or, if you have already made up your mind, it will enable you to present an effective counter-argument (more on this later).

ACTIVITY 2

In the table below are opinions on '**Watching television is bad for you**'; beside them are some ideas you might consider to challenge these points.

Working in groups, consider what points you could raise to challenge or question the last three points.

POINTS YOU'VE BEEN GIVEN	ANALYSIS
• Watching television kills conversation.	Watching television could give rise to conversations between family and friends about programmes watched.
• A range of educational programmes is shown.	Are there enough of these types of programmes? Many of the programmes contain bad language, violence and sexually explicit material. Is this educational?
• Television provides instant access to news and other information.	There are other ways of accessing the news, such as radio, the Internet and newspapers. Could images shown desensitise us to violence and bloodshed?
• Television discourages play amongst young people.	
• Television advertising puts unfair pressure on consumers	
• Television programmes are entertaining.	

Now repeat this process on the points you came up with yourself.

4 Organising your ideas

After you have analysed the points given as well as your own, it is time to organise your ideas.

You should sort out what you consider to be the most important point in your discussion. Then you could move on to the next most significant one, and so on. You might find at this stage you decide to leave out some of the points you came up with during your brainstorming session.

It is possible to number these so that they provide you with the paragraph running order for your essay.

ACTIVITY 3

Using the points given and those you came up with yourself for the statement, '**Watching television is bad for you**', organise the order in which you could address these points. Consider which should come first and how your points are going to flow into each other. Do this individually before explaining your choices to another student.

5 Structuring your response

There is a range of possible ways to structure your essay. You might choose to start by stating your point of view on the subject, and the rest of your essay could then be composed of your analysis of the topic. Or you may choose to consider your range of discussion points about the given statement and then come to your own conclusion.

If you decide to argue a particular way, either for or against the statement, it is vital that you show your reader that you are aware of the other side of the argument. This shows the examiner you are aware of alternative viewpoints to your own and that you have analysed the topic thoroughly.

This technique is known as using a **counter-argument**. To exploit it effectively it is important to have challenged the points you have assembled before beginning to write your essay.

---

6 Supporting evidence

Once you have organised your points it is important to think of evidence to support them. This will make your case more convincing and your writing appear more assured. You can use evidence from a range of sources:

▸ **Personal experience (anecdote)** – Sometimes including a brief account of something that has happened in your life, or the life of someone you know, can make your argument more interesting and convincing. For example:

You may think mobile phones are a nuisance, but my mobile phone saved my life! It was a Friday evening in December; it was raining heavily and already quite dark. I was walking home from school, and was just about to cross the road when all of a sudden...

▸ **Books, television and film** – You may well have watched a film, television programme, or have read a book that is relevant to the topic you are discussing. Do not be afraid to draw on your experience of these to support your argument. For example:

The novel Junk by Melvin Burgess is a depressing and pessimistic account of the dangers teenagers face when they become involved in drug abuse.

or

A recent Channel 4 documentary called 'Sorted' interviewed a range of young people about their experiences with drugs. Over fifty per cent of those interviewed claimed they had either taken or been offered illegal drugs.

▶ **Facts and figures** – Relevant facts and figures can make your argument sound convincing. They show you are well informed about the topic you are discussing. (Clearly you will be fortunate to be able to draw upon this source in the exam.) For example:

98% of all UK households have a television set.

or

The Royal College of Veterinary Surgeons believes that hunting with hounds is the most natural and humane way of controlling the fox population in the countryside.

However, you should **avoid making generalisations** in your writing. A generalisation is a form of sweeping statement that is not always true. For example:

All footballers are really wealthy.

Using this sort of supporting evidence will only weaken the case you are trying to make.

ACTIVITY 4

Make a **plan** for an essay based on the question below.

Present your views on the following statement:

Exams should be abolished.

Below is a range of issues related to the issue of exams. The examiner wants you to review the points that you consider to be important, along with any ideas of your own. Analyse these in an extended piece of writing. You will be expected to include your own comments and conclusions on the topic.

▶ *They only test bits of the course – you can hit it lucky.*
▶ Use of assignments and coursework is a fairer way of assessing.
▶ *I work hard during the year, but I just can't do exams!*
▶ At least with an exam everybody gets the same chance!

Your plan should include:
▶ points in favour of the statement
▶ points against the statement
▶ ideas for evidence to support your points.

Organising your plan

a   Consider how you will structure your essay. Are you going to argue for or against the statement, or are you going to adopt a balanced approach?

b   Which point will come first?

c How will the next point lead on from the one before?

After you have finished your plan, read over the running order of your points. Check that they are:

▸ relevant and related to the question

▸ organised so that you can follow them.

Remember you will need to plan your essay **before** beginning to write. However, do not be afraid to add to your plan or change it as you are writing.

7 Writing the essay

At this stage you should know what points will be included in your essay and where every part of it is going to go. Now it is time to get down to the business of writing it.

The introduction

A powerful introduction is important for any essay. Remember first impressions are very important. An introduction should not be too long. Instead, you should get to the point right away. Your introduction is the place where you first alert your reader to the issue you are discussing and possibly state your position on it.

There are a number of ways you could make your introduction interesting and effective. Here are a few of the techniques that you could choose from:

▸ Find some common ground. This is a powerful way to bring your reader over to your side. There is usually some area upon which all reasonable people agree, often a common goal:

All of us know how seriously some people treat the game of football.

▸ Open strongly with an original statement:

Football killed my fish!

▸ Give some background information on the statement:

The modern game of football dates back to the twelfth century.

▸ You could be provocative:

Watching football makes you boring!

▸ Be balanced, showing awareness of both sides of the argument:

Many people are passionate about football but others find the game and its supporters incredibly boring.

▸ You could begin with a quotation on the subject:

It was Pele who first called soccer 'the beautiful game'.

▸ Use an anecdote:

I was six when I first saw Arsenal play...

▸ Offer a direct statement:

Football is a game that involves two teams of eleven players...

▸ Ask a rhetorical question:

Have you ever thought about what life would be like without football?

ACTIVITY 5

Identify what types of techniques are used in the following introductions.

a. *I was only six when I first visited the zoo, but even then at that young age I knew it was wrong to keep animals locked up in cages.*

b. *Some people love the excitement and buzz of living in the city, however, for others city life is too fast, too noisy and too dangerous.*

c. *We all care about the future of our planet.*

d. *Animal experimentation is evil.*

e. *Do you hate your school uniform?*

Remember these are only the beginnings to your introduction; you will have to add to them. By the end of the introduction you should have aroused the interest of your reader and introduced them to the subject, and you may have indicated your view on it.

ACTIVITY 6

Now write three different types of introduction for an essay on the title '**Watching television is bad for you**'.

Paragraphing

When planning your essay you came up with a range of different points. Each one of these points should be placed in a **separate** paragraph.

At this stage it might be useful to remind yourself of what a paragraph is. A paragraph is a series of sentences that are organised and are all related to a single topic.

Paragraphs can contain many different kinds of information. Regardless of the kind of information they contain, all paragraphs share certain characteristics. One of the most important of these is the **topic sentence**.

A topic sentence is usually placed at the beginning of your paragraph. The topic sentence will introduce the main idea of the paragraph; it will summarise and give an overview of what the paragraph is about. The rest of the paragraph will then explain, develop or support with evidence the topic sentence's main idea or claim. The topic sentence is usually the first sentence of a paragraph, but not necessarily: it may come at the end of a paragraph.

Here is an example of a topic sentence and how it functions as a signpost for the rest of the paragraph.

Skateboarding is not recognised as a proper sport. Most towns will have sports facilities such as football grounds, gymnasiums, and ice rinks that cater for a wide range of sporting interests. Yet very few towns possess skate parks. This means that skateboarders often end up skating in urban areas; however, their presence seems to incense others in the community. Police or local shop owners see them as a threat to their property and will try to move them on. Members of the public regard them as noisy and antisocial; there is little attempt to understand that what they are doing is highly skilled and takes lots of practice. There is just as much talent involved in 'popping an ollie' as there is in making a hole in one or scoring a winning goal.

ACTIVITY 7

In each case select the relevant topic sentence for the paragraph that follows.

a

▸ Zoos have an educational role.
▸ Animals in zoos suffer.
▸ Visiting the zoo can be an enjoyable experience.

Zoos are places where people can go to learn about different types of animals. As well as learning about animals you also get the opportunity to see them up close. This experience is better than anything you could ever read about or see on television.

b

▸ Looking after a pet can be expensive.
▸ You need to be responsible to look after a pet.
▸ Pets can make good companions.

There are many issues to consider. Can you spare enough time? You need to make sure you are able to play with them and clean up after them. Then, of course, there is the financial side of things to consider, as owning a pet can be an expensive business. You need to supply them with a bed and food, and make sure they have regular check-ups with the vet.

c

▸ Some sporting celebrities are more interested in advertising designer gear than playing their sport.
▸ Professional sportsmen and sportswomen have only a brief career.
▸ Top stars are constantly pestered by the media.

They have to make the most of their time in the spotlight. They cannot afford to turn down the financial deals offered to them by the major sportswear companies. If they do so, they may not get another chance, as in a few years' time their sporting career may be over.

d
> A big win on the National Lottery could ruin your life.
> Winning the Lottery could change your life.
> The Lottery generates a lot of money for good causes.

Family members can all too easily end up feuding over who gets what and this makes other people's lives miserable. Sometimes people cannot manage their money and within a matter of years families have lost the money they won. In the cases of these Lottery winners, money certainly does not buy happiness.

ACTIVITY 8

Now go back to your plan for the essay on exams. Write a topic sentence for each of the paragraphs you intend to use in your essay.

Using linguistic devices

For most of us, these rather complicated-sounding terms are not important in themselves but the functions that they perform are worth understanding and using.

Discursive markers

These are words and phrases which, if used correctly, can add fluency to your writing and help you to link ideas and paragraphs together. They will help your response develop in a logical and structured way. Try using the following discursive markers to:

> show the results of a point you have made:
> *Consequently   Therefore   Furthermore   As a result   Thus*

> show a shift in your argument:
> *However   Despite this   In opposition to this   Nevertheless   On the other hand*
> *Another way   Another view is   Even though   In spite of this   In the meantime*
> *Unlike this   Alternatively   In contrast to this   At the same time   Yet*
> *Although   Even so*

> show order:
> *Initially   In the first place   In the second place   Lastly   Finally*

> show you are coming to a conclusion:
> *Eventually   `Finally   To conclude   To summarise*
> *At last   To sum up   In conclusion*

> introduce examples:
> *An example of this   For instance   To illustrate this*

> introduce a comparison or similarity:
> *Accordingly   In keeping with this   Similarly   Just as*
> *Similar to this   In comparison to this   Likewise*

Rhetorical devices

You can use rhetorical devices in your writing to engage, influence and persuade your reader to agree with your position. Below is a range of common rhetorical devices.

▸ **Lists of three** – Listing things in groups of three adds weight and impact to your comment, making it an effective way of getting your point across.

I combine the three least useful qualities for a sports person – I'm big, slow and weak

Boxing is a noble, skilful and entertaining sport.

▸ **Rhetorical questions** – These are questions that are designed to involve and challenge the reader. They are asked for effect rather than to call for an answer. The answer is usually quite obvious.

Who wouldn't want to earn as much money as a film star?

Can any civilisation justify being so cruel?

▸ **Contrasts** – This is a good way of emphasising the significance of the point you are making.

What are regarded as some of the best video games can sometimes bring out the very worst in the people who play them.

That's one small step for man, one giant leap for mankind.

▸ **Emotive language** – This can help you to put your point across in a powerful and convincing manner.

Can you imagine the sheer torture these animals have to endure?

Boxing is a cruel and barbaric sport.

▸ **Repetition** – This is a good way of emphasising your point.

A great people has been moved to defend a great nation.

What is important is education, education, education!

Note: Avoid using 'you' and try to use 'we' and 'us'. This will make your readers feel that they are on your side. It will also make the readers feel you are addressing them personally and so involve them more in your response.

The conclusion

Conclusions are just as important as introductions. You should not introduce a new point in your conclusion. Instead your conclusion should summarise your stance and main points. If possible your last sentence should be one that encourages your reader to think about the topic that you have just been discussing. You could do this by asking a question, calling for some kind of action or warning of what could happen. For example:

Finally, I believe we need to continue funding space exploration. It is possible that one day our world will be overcrowded and we will need to expand to find alternative living spaces. Without the information we receive from space exploration the possibility of relocating to other planets will be closed to us. If we do not support space exploration today, we could live to regret it, as what we could be jeopardising is the very future of the entire human race.

However, if you can see the reasons for and against do not be afraid to end on a balanced note:

To conclude, I believe that there are many good reasons why we should support space exploration. It enables us to learn more about our world and our universe and this information could be used to ensure the survival of the human race. Despite this, I am also aware of the reasons why some people have expressed concern over the vast amounts of money being spent every year on space exploration. It is my belief that we should continue to finance space exploration, but only if we begin to pay more attention to the problems faced by many people in our own and other countries.

Points to remember about conclusions

▸ Refer to the question again.
▸ Include a brief summary of the main points.
▸ Don't introduce a new idea in your conclusion.
▸ You can end by:
  ● asking a provocative question
  ● calling for some sort of action
  ● presenting a warning
  ● suggesting potential results or consequences.

8 Style

Knowing that your audience is the examiner helps you to select an appropriate style. Aim to write in standard formal English. Be reasonable and logical; however, you can use emotive language to show that you feel strongly about the issue. Your writing should be lively and show evidence of engagement with the task, but avoid being over-familiar or using inappropriate language such as slang.

Getting the style of your writing right is quite hard. It is important to think about the type of topic you are discussing. If it is a very serious topic then humour will not be appropriate. If, however, you can appropriately use moments of humour then you will certainly be credited for them. Avoid writing in an angry or overly aggressive style. Instead, carefully choose words that reveal the strength of your feelings.

At all times you should aim to be polite. When criticising opinions other than your own, avoid becoming personal. For example:

I think anyone who supports boxing is no better than an animal.

Remember this essay can reflect your personal opinion, therefore, do not be afraid to use words and phrases such as:

I think it's only fair...

I strongly support...

I certainly feel...

My view on this point is...

I hope I have convinced you...

---

9 Technical accuracy

Check your writing

You should also give yourself some time at the end of your writing to check over your work for technical accuracy. Remember that in this section of the exam one-third of the available marks will be awarded for your sentence structure, spelling and punctuation.

Sentences

Make sure all sentences are correctly punctuated. Check for full stops. Are your sentences too long or too short? Remember the occasional short sentence can be dramatic and effective. For instance:

We all know that exercise is good for us and we frequently watch advertisements on the television which urge us to take sensible exercise. I do. I change channels immediately!

ACTIVITY 9

What is the effect of the longer sentence at the start? What is the effect of the two shorter sentences at the end?

Paragraphs

Check that each paragraph covers only one point. Do your paragraphs have a topic sentence? Do the paragraphs flow from one into the other? Have you used discursive markers to improve the flow from one paragraph to another?

Commas and apostrophes

When you are revising, remind yourself of the rules for using apostrophes and commas. Now check that there are not too may commas or perhaps worse, none at all! Check that all your apostrophes are in the right place.

Vocabulary

Try to use as varied, appropriate and wide a range of words as possible.

Words should be spelt correctly. Pay particular attention to those words that you use quite often and that cause you difficulty. It would be a good idea to create your own spelling log, where you list (and check up on and learn) your problem spellings.

Handwriting

Your handwriting should allow you to write reasonably quickly yet at the same time it should be legible.

10 Time to get practical

In the second section of this book, you have learnt the skills required in answering the type of essay question that appears in CCEA's GCSE English, Paper 1 Section B. It is important that you practise these skills on a realistic task and preferably under examination conditions. In the actual examination, you will only have **one hour** for this section of the paper.

Below is a series of key points to use as a revision checklist.

▸ Always **think** and **plan**, and only then **write**!

▸ Remember the examiner is your audience; therefore write in standard English using quite a formal style. This does not mean that the examiner wants to be treated to a very dry, formal piece of writing. There is room for personal engagement, humour or irony in your writing!

▸ Organise your points **before** beginning to write – spend at least ten minutes planning and organising.

▸ Make sure you add to the points offered and develop them appropriately.

▸ Don't be afraid to disagree with the given statement.

▸ Include an introduction and conclusion.

▸ Make sure each point has a separate paragraph.

▸ Use evidence to support your points.

▸ Use counter-arguments to show you have considered alternative points of view.

▸ Use a variety of sentences to keep your writing interesting.

▸ Stick to the point.

▸ Never insult your reader by being impolite or threatening. Avoid suggesting that other viewpoints are 'silly' or 'foolish' (or worse!).

▸ Do not generalise.

▸ Spend about five minutes at the end re-reading what you have written. Alter any sentences that do not make sense. Check your paragraphing. Correct any spelling mistakes you come across.

The two test pieces that follow are typical of Paper 1 Section B.

FOUNDATION TIER SAMPLE PAPER

Paper 1   Section B

This section tests **writing**: to review, analyse and comment.

- Write in a way that suits this type of task.

- To answer the question effectively you should aim to write **at least two sides**.

- Leave enough time to **reread your work** so that you can make any changes you feel necessary.

Present your views on the following statement:

Computer games are harmful to children.

The opinions listed below raise a series of issues about the effects of computer games on children. The examiner wants you to review the issues that you consider to be important along with any ideas of your own. Analyse these in an extended piece of writing. You will be expected to include your own comments and conclusions on the topic.

- Computer games are educational – they develop your ability to think and plan strategically.

- *They can make young people become more violent*.

- They encourage you to be more imaginative.

- *They are bad for your health – nintendo thumb, repetitive strain injury and bad posture are all examples of the injuries caused by computer games*.

- They are harmless fun.

- *Some people can become addicted to computer games*.

[30 marks]

HIGHER TIER SAMPLE PAPER

Paper 1   Section B

This section tests **writing**: to review, analyse and comment.

- Write in a way that suits this type of task.

- To answer the question effectively you should aim to write **at least two sides**.

- Leave enough time to **reread your work** so that you can make any changes you feel necessary.

Present your views on the following statement:

Computer games are harmful to children.

The opinions listed below raise a series of issues about the effects of computer games on children. The examiner wants you to review the issues that you consider to be important along with any ideas of your own. Analyse these in an extended piece of writing. You will be expected to include your own comments and conclusions on the topic.

- Computer games are educational – they develop your ability to think and plan strategically.

- *They can make young people become more violent*.

- They are harmless fun.

- *They are bad for your health – nintendo thumb, repetitive strain injury and bad posture are all examples of the injuries caused by computer games*.

[30 marks]

PAPER 2
SECTION A
Writing to inform, explain and describe

THE ASSESSMENT OBJECTIVES

These are the skills and abilities that this **writing** section tests.

The percentage of the marks given to the different assessment objectives

66.66%

Students are expected to show the ability to:

a put across what has to be said in a clear and original way

b take note of the purpose and the target audience, and use a writing form that suits both

c organise ideas into sentences and paragraphs

d make use of language and structure techniques to create the desired effect

e present work clearly and neatly

33.33%

f use a range of sentence structures effectively

g punctuate accurately

h spell accurately.

...ities such as football grounds, gymnasiums, and ice rinks that cater for...
...de range of sporting interests. Yet very few towns possess skate parks. This me...
...at skateboarders often end up skating in urban areas; however, their prese...
...ems to incense others in the community. Police or local shop owners see th...
...a threat to their property and will try to move them on. Members of the...
...blic regard them as noisy and antisocial; there is little attempt to...
...stand that what they are doing is highly skilled and takes a lot...

1 What's required?

The kinds of task you will meet in your examination will ask you to write about something familiar to you, something that you can develop from your own experience – from school or college events, or from experiences of life at home or with your friends. You will be expected to **inform** the reader about your subject matter, and to **explain** and **describe** it.

You will be asked to write within a particular form, such as an article, a speech, a letter or a personal essay.

Your immediate audience will be the examiner, but the examiner will be assessing how well you have directed your writing towards the specific audience for whom you have been asked to write.

2 Background preparation

You need to find opportunities to broaden your reading experience in these forms of writing. By doing this, you will gather ideas and also experience of how these kinds of writing work. You need to experience the style of a range of writers and you will see in action the devices and techniques they use.

Where to look

Magazines and newspapers are the main places to look for writing that aims to inform, explain and describe. Sunday newspapers, with all their different sections, are particularly useful.

Look out for the travel section; the food section; the regular column, in which a writer gives their opinion; the letters page; the sports section and the magazine section, in which you often find a columnist offering elements of autobiography as well as his/her opinion.

From this private reading you will find that a writer needs to plan:
▸ to inform you by organising the facts
▸ to explain by organising his/her ideas and opinions
▸ to describe by using language to create what he/she has seen or experienced.

Another thing that you will pick up from this reading on your own is that people write letters and articles about events and enthusiasms in their own lives. A very important element in this kind of writing is the sharing of an enthusiasm.

3 Injecting enthusiasm into your writing

Food, glorious food!

Many newspapers and magazines have a section in which a writer writes about food. The writer may be trying to encourage you to try a particular kind of food before giving you some recipes, or he/she may be describing the experience of eating a particular food – as in the following series of examples.

ACTIVITY 1

Look at the way cookery writer Nigel Slater conveys his enthusiasm for everyday foods.

What is it about eating a hot potato that makes me feel so good? Yes, of course, it is the most comforting and sustaining food of all, not to mention cheap and easy to come by, but there has to be more to it than that. Is it that when rubbed with salt and baked in the oven, a plump potato warms me like nothing else? Could it be the way its flesh soaks up cream and garlic in a gratin, or mashes so blissfully with butter? Might it be the way its outside crisps and shines when roasted round the Sunday joint while its inside stays moist and gooey?

From 'The Hot Potato' by Nigel Slater

Let's look at the effect upon the reader of his use of certain techniques.

▸ **Questions** – These are to the point – in your face you might say. The effect allows the writer to speak very directly to the reader and as a result we are immediately caught up, almost as if we were in conversation with the writer.

▸ **Examples** – Our imaginations work so much better if they have examples to help us picture in our mind's eye what the writer is talking about. We can all visualise 'a hot potato' or 'the way its outside crisps'.

▸ **Particular words and phrases** – The use of descriptive words and phrases bring to life the real sense of these tasty delights – 'the *plump* potato' or '*soaks* up cream' or '*mashes so blissfully* with butter'.

ACTIVITY 2

Of course potatoes may not be your favourite food. Try some of his chicken instead.

A big, fat, free range chicken is a magnificent thing to unwrap on your return from the shops. Full of promise. We can butter it with generosity, tuck tufts of thyme and bay leaves under its legs and let it roast until its skin is crisp; or we can cut it up and leave it to bubble quietly with mushrooms, cream and wine, or slap it on the bars of a hot grill and brush it with tarragon, mustard and garlic till it shines and sizzles.

From 'Real Chicken' by Nigel Slater

Here we can see the writer again using some of the same techniques that he used when discussing potatoes. In addition, however, some different techniques are employed.

Consider the effect upon the reader of his use of:

a the image of unwrapping

b the word 'we'

c alliteration

d the verb 'slap'

e lists.

ACTIVITY 3

If you can't get enthusiastic about potatoes or chicken, try chocolate.

How horrible it would be to live in a world without chocolate. A world devoid of the strings of sticky caramel in a Mars Bar; the crisp snap of a square of the finest Valrhona; the feel of a pale Flake as it dissolves on the tongue; and the hot-cold sensation of warm chocolate sauce on a cold vanilla ice cream. Chocolate runs through my life like a comfort blanket; a teddy bear you can eat.

From 'A World without Chocolate' by Nigel Slater

What is the effect upon the reader of the writer's use of:

a brand names such as Mars Bar and Flake?

b the detailed description of what each different kind of chocolate feels like to eat?

c the images of the comfort blanket and the teddy bear?

ACTIVITY 4

Most of us have favourite foods, and food writing can provide an ideal way to practise informing the reader about your favourite food, explaining why you enjoy that food so much and describing the pleasure of cooking or eating your favourite food.

Your college magazine has decided to ask one of the teachers, one of the students and one of the non-teaching staff to write a 300-word article about their favourite food. You are the student who has been asked.

Plan your article in three parts.

a   Inform your reader about your favourite food.
b   Explain why you enjoy this food so much.
c   Describe your experience of enjoying your favourite food.

You will need to plan a conclusion that will help the reader to share your enthusiasm. You could tell them about the shops in which to find the very best examples of your favourite food, or you could encourage them to try different ways of preparing or cooking your favourite food.

4 Generating interest

Faraway places

The travel section of a newspaper or magazine is also a good place to look for examples of writers informing, explaining or describing their experiences on holidays or journeys.

ACTIVITY 5

A travel section about Australia in a Sunday paper will usually encourage you to go to the exciting city of Sydney. In the following article, Jeremy Atiyah sets out to share his enthusiasm for Australia's very different and very much smaller capital city, Canberra.

If a scattering of buildings in a leafy meadow can qualify as a city, Canberra qualifies. But it makes more sense, I admit, to describe the capital of Australia as a kind of garden; as a city, after all, it hasn't really got started. Founded 89 years ago, hardly any of it had been built until well into the Fifties, but as a garden of golden grass, dried creeks and giant ants' nests, it is one of the most ancient beauty spots on earth.

It is not sexy like Sydney, but it is still desirable. Instead of traffic jams and road rage, Canberrans make do with shady lawns and avenues of gum trees and flowering shrubs. Driving here over the mountains from Sydney, you are scarcely aware that you have entered a city at all until you see a sign announcing that you have reached the centre. You push foliage aside in search of tarmac and concrete, and see exotic birds swooping about in pine trees. Hardly anyone is wearing a suit, but plenty are in shorts and sandals.

The background noise is not of cars but of crickets and warm winds swooshing in the leaves. Flaking bark crackles underfoot. the scent of gum resin and dry herbs fills the air. Ants still have more impact on the environment of this so-called city than human beings.

Traditionally people have laughed at Canberra for lacking culture or urban vibrancy: it is a dull, planned city of bureaucrats and administrators and landscape gardeners, they say, not a living, organic city of artists or creative people. Its streets are lined with trees planted by colonial officials. It may be the city least touched by history in the entire world. Notions such as war or invasion or revolution do not spring to mind in the context of Canberra. What, in fact, has ever happened here, beyond the construction of a few roads and sewerage lines, plus government offices and homes for civil servants?

But this is to miss the point. Instead of arts and popular entertainment, the residents of this city have yellow-winged grasshoppers skimming their lawns, sulphur-

crested cockatoos perching on their verandahs, peach trees shedding their fruit in their swimming pools. Beyond this, Canberra needs artificial entertainments in the same measure as it needs traffic jams or road rage.

So, why bother with tinselly places like Sydney, I ask myself, when the quintessential Australian city lies here, deep in the bush, affixed to a one-million-year-old landscape?

From 'Postcard from Canberra' by Jeremy Atiyah

You can see that the writer has been faced with a difficult task in trying to persuade readers that Canberra is worth a visit instead of Sydney, or one of the other Australian cities. The writer thinks that most readers will know very little about Canberra, and sets out to inform us. He feels that he has to make a case to prove that Canberra is just as worth visiting as the other cities. The writer hopes to describe Canberra in a way that will arouse our curiosity and help us understand his enthusiasm for this small city.

What is the effect upon the reader of the writer's skills in:

a telling us the bad things first?

b including Australian words with which we may be unfamiliar?

c using a turning point in the line 'But this is to miss the point'?
d using comparison and contrast?

ACTIVITY 6

Your local council has launched a competition in which people living in your area have been asked to write about your part of the world in a way that would make it attractive for visitors.

You are asked to write an article in which you:
▸ inform your readers about the area
▸ explain why you feel the area is worth a visit
▸ describe some of the attractions.

You will need to plan a strong conclusion. You will be aware that many areas in Northern Ireland are trying to attract visitors. You might plan to finish your article with a paragraph in which you compare and contrast your area with other places to which a visitor might go.

5 Using your own experience and expertise

Hobbies and interests

You will also find articles by authors who are writing in order to share their enthusiasm for a hobby, sport or other interest. Most of us have an interest that means a lot to us and which we could write about enthusiastically in order to gain the reader's interest.

Read the following article in which Justine Hankins shares her enthusiasm for pet rabbits, which can sometimes seem very boring as pets.

Home for most rabbits was once a pen in the garden but now the UK's third most popular pet is hopping freely...around the living room. Help yourself to carrot cake, because today we're celebrating International Rabbit Day. The annual event is planned by the Rabbit Charity, an organisation dedicated to spreading the word about bunnies. The message is simple: rabbits are 'intelligent, affectionate, entertaining and sensitive creatures'.

I wouldn't dream of suggesting otherwise, but let's face it, rabbits are generally regarded as B-list pets – a long way behind cats and dogs, those elite creatures that sleep on the bed, get taken on holiday, receive expert medical care and even birthday and Christmas presents; in many cases, they're regarded with greater fondness than human members of the family. Rabbits, however, despite being the nation's third most popular pet, rarely enjoy such attention, and not usually for a lifetime. The life expectancy of a rabbit is seven to ten years, but pet rabbits often fall out of favour long before then. Many rabbits lead a lonely existence in tiny hutches at the bottom of the garden; adorable, then boring, then neglected. More than 30,000 end up in rescue centres every year.

But there are signs that Thumper is coming in from the cold. More and more people are keeping rabbits in the home, where they can hop around freely. There was a time when no one over 12 would admit to loving a bunny. Not any more. The 'house rabbit' trend, which started in the US in the 1980s, is often an adult passion. These days, pet shops are crammed with special toys and treats for bunnies. Your bunny can live in an elaborate designer hutch when at home and while you're away he can stay in a luxury bunny hotel.

Rabbits also have fans among the marginally famous. Suggs, Toyah Willcox and the head of design at Habitat, Tom Dixon, have all publicly praised their house bunnies. Petplan introduced rabbit insurance policies in 1998, in response to public demand, and there have been significant improvements in the veterinary treatment available to them.

Petplan estimates that one out of five rabbits live indoors. The Rabbit Charity would like to see far more bunnies living free-range in our homes and is against hutches altogether. The organisation's director, Caroline James, says her bunnies are happy to sleep in a dog basket and recommends using a baby gate if you need to confine your rabbit to one room. The Rabbit Welfare Association is fine with hutches for indoor or outdoor use, so long as they're big. A hutch should be large enough to allow a rabbit to stand upright, and they also need enough space for regular exercise. Many of the hutches on sale in pet shops are simply too small.

Any rabbit would be happier exploring the living room than shut in a hutch. But is it really wise to have a rabbit on the loose? Possibly not, but wisdom doesn't really come into it. After all, cats and dogs can be a terrible nuisance, but we don't keep them in cages. Rabbits love to chew and burrow, and can be very destructive in a home that is not adequately bunny-proofed. Electric cables, telephone wires and carpets will all need to be protected.

The good news is that bunnies can be litter trained without too much difficulty. They are also very affectionate and surprisingly bold. They're so sociable, in fact, that you should really have at least two – but you may need to get the vet to have a little chat with them about family planning.

Contact the Rabbit Charity on 020-89880001 (therabbitcharity.freeserve.co.uk). The Rabbit Welfare Association, call 01403 277658 (rabbitwelfare.com).

From 'Beyond the Hutch' by Justine Hankins

The writer seems to know that most readers will think that a cat or a dog would be a much more acceptable pet.

What is the effect upon the reader of the writer's use of:

a   the details given about the lives of pet cats and dogs ?

b   the use of the word 'bunny' and 'bunnies', and the name 'Thumper'?

c the details from the pet insurance company Petplan?

d the mention of celebrities such as Suggs, Toyah Willcox and Tom Dixon?

e the conclusion?

ACTIVITY 7

You have been asked to write a letter about one of your particular interests or enthusiasms to a class of students your own age at your twin school in Canada.

You will need a plan in order to ensure that you:

▸ inform your readers about your enthusiasm

▸ explain why you find your enthusiasm so rewarding

▸ describe your enthusiasm in a way that readers can share.

You will need to realise that Canada is a very different country with a very different culture, and you will have to work hard to ensure that your twin class really understand your enthusiasm.

6 Planning and structuring your piece of writing

ACTIVITY 8

Choose one of the following tasks:

a Write a personal essay for the examiner in which you explain the importance of friendship and the part your friends play in your life.

b Write an article for your school or college magazine in which you describe your experience of journeying somewhere for the first time.

Before you start to write, it is important to consider the planning issues that either of these pieces of writing require.

In planning your essay about friendship, would you begin:

▸ by introducing your best friend or your group of friends in order to emphasise that friends are important to you?

▸ by writing about the importance of friendship in order to show that friendship is a topic of interest to everyone?

▸ by writing about famous friendships in order to engage the examiner's interest?

In planning your piece of travel writing, would you begin:

▸ with an attention-grabbing title?

▸ at the moment when you saw something new and amazing, in order to grab the reader's attention?

▶ at the start of your journey, in order to give the reader the feeling of travelling along with you?

▶ with your memory of the journey, in order to emphasise that the experience has stayed in your memory?

For each piece of writing you need to be very clear about the **purpose** and the **audience** for which it is written. When you read over a working draft, ask yourself whether you have achieved your purpose and have addressed your audience. In the case of the essay on friendship, have you explained to the examiner why you believe friendship is important? For the travel-writing piece, have you described for the school or college reader the essential experiences of your journey? Remember, the examiner will be considering how well you have directed your writing towards the audience specified by your writing task.

In the case of each piece of writing, you will need to plan. It might be useful to look back at the work you did in Paper 1 Section B. Much of what you learnt and practised about planning and developing your writing will be useful here.

For your piece of personal writing on friendship you may need connectives (words or phrases used to help link ideas within and between paragraphs) that draw attention to your point of view. Here are some examples:

As a consequence of   An upshot of   An outcome of   As a result of

For your travel article, you may need connectives that emphasise time and place, and also allow you to draw attention to your personal reaction to the experience of the journey. Here are some examples:

Finally   Soon   Afterwards   On another occasion

Chronology (the order of things) may also be important. You need to show an awareness of the order in which events happen. However, you may decide to change the chronology for effect, say by structuring your travel piece so that you mention the most memorable experience at the beginning, rather than the first thing you saw.

The important thing is to offer information, explanation or description in an order that will engage your audience and achieve your purpose. You need to structure your text in a way that will take account of your audience and grab their attention.

You will already have begun to develop your own methods of planning a piece of writing. Here are some examples:

a   You might decide that because a particular task has two purposes (for example, you have been asked to write a letter to a friend describing your arrangements for a train journey around Europe in order to see a series of historic cities) a plan set out in two columns might be a good idea:

ARRANGEMENTS	HIGHLIGHTS

Once you have planned your two columns, and you are sure that you have sorted out the material so that it will achieve its purpose, you can decide which set of information to give first. You can justify starting with either the arrangements or the highlights. However, it would probably be sensible not to mix the two sections so that your friend – the audience – will be able to refer back to your letter if they need to look up the arrangements, or want to have an idea of what to look forward to. You will probably wish your letter to be welcoming, and to end on a friendly and enthusiastic note.

b Your piece of personal writing would probably best be planned using a spider diagram so that you can let your ideas build up. There is no practical reason to start with one idea rather than another. Once you have brainstormed all the issues and examples you wish to cover in an essay about friendship, you can plan the order of your paragraphs according to what you think will grab the reader's attention.

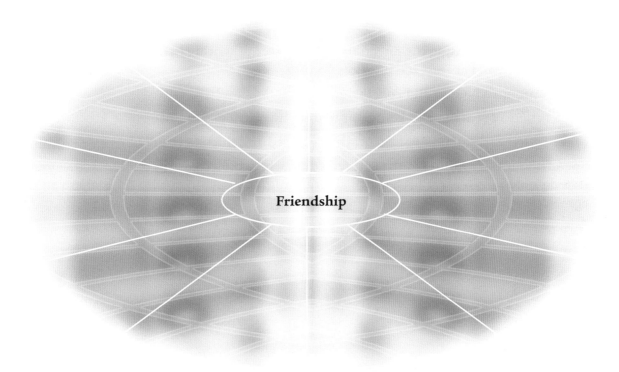

Friendship

Your audience, the examiner, will be interested in how important friendship is to you. You could start with your own friendships, you might start with some examples of famous friendships that have stood the test of time, only bringing in examples and personal experience once you have grabbed the examiner's attention.

c You might use a timeline to plan your travel piece about your journey. The timeline will include all the major sights and experiences you wish to include. However, a common mistake in planning a piece of writing about a journey is to start at the beginning of the journey and give equal attention to everything that you saw. Once you have set out your timeline, you can decide what the really memorable experiences were, and the sights and sounds you would like to recreate in your description. Boring bits of the journey don't need to be mentioned.

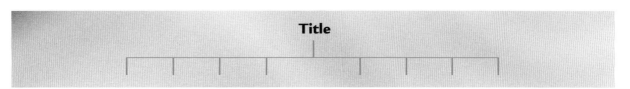

Title

7 Time to get practical

In the third section of this book, you have learnt the skills required in answering the type of question that appears in Paper 2 Section A. It is important that you practise these skills on a realistic task and preferably under examination conditions. In the actual examination, you will only have **one hour** for this section of the paper.

Below is a series of key points to use as a revision checklist.

- Always **think** and **plan**, and only then **write**!
- Remember to keep the **purpose** for your writing at the forefront of your thinking.
- Keep your **audience** in mind throughout – make sure your writing is appropriate for its intended audience.
- Planning and organising the direction of your piece of writing **before** beginning to write is essential. Spend **at least ten minutes** on this.
- Include an introduction and conclusion.
- Use a variety of sentences to keep your writing interesting.
- Make sure the paragraphing is logically organised and fluently handled.
- Spend about **five minutes** at the end rereading what you have written. Alter any sentences that do not make sense. Check your paragraphing. Correct any spelling mistakes you come across.

The two test pieces that follow are typical of Paper 2 Section A.

FOUNDATION TIER SAMPLE PAPER

Paper 2   Section A

This section tests **writing**: to inform, explain and describe.

- Write in a way that suits this type of task.

- To answer the question effectively you should aim to write **at least two sides**.

- Leave enough time to **reread your work** so that you can make any changes you feel necessary.

'My proudest moment!' Write an account for the examiner of the most important achievement in your life.

In your account, you should:

- explain what you had to do

- inform the examiner about the other people involved (if any)

- describe your thoughts and feelings about it all.

[30 marks]

HIGHER TIER SAMPLE PAPER

Paper 2   Section A

This section tests **writing**: to inform, explain and describe.

- Write in a way that suits this type of task.

- To answer the question effectively you should aim to write **at least two sides**.

- Leave enough time to **reread your work** so that you can make any changes you feel necessary.

Recently, a very special guest visited your school or college. Write a lively and informative article for your school or college magazine, describing this event.

In your article you should:

- explain who the guest was and the reason(s) for the visit

- inform the reader of the preparations made

- describe the main events of the visit.

[30 marks]

PAPER 2
SECTION B
Reading: Response to non-fiction and media texts

THE ASSESSMENT OBJECTIVES

These are the skills and abilities that this **reading** section tests.

The percentage of the marks given to the different assessment objectives

100%

Students are expected to show the ability to:

a read with insight and engagement

b select suitable points from a text

c note the difference between fact and opinion, and consider how information is presented

d follow a series of reasons put forward to support a case, and consider the strengths and weaknesses of the argument

e examine material from different texts and make cross-references

f understand and assess how writers use language and structure to bring about their desired effects.

1 What's required?

The examiner is assessing your ability to demonstrate an understanding of **how** two writers have:

▶ developed their outlook on a particular topic
▶ used particular forms of writing.

You will be required to cross-reference and compare aspects of the text as well as assessing the techniques they have used and the effectiveness of their writing.

The strategies and methods used by writers

Before considering how you are expected to analyse these texts, it is logical to start by taking a detailed look at the ways writers go about the business of developing these forms of writing.

You will be learning how writers:

a make use of fact and opinion
b present information and develop a point of view
c structure their work and their methods of presentation
d use words and phrases.

What is meant by non-fiction and media texts?

You probably know what **non-fiction** and **media** texts are but in case you have forgotten or don't know, let's begin with clearing up what is meant by these terms.

A **non-fiction text** is simply a piece of writing that is not made up – it has its basis in fact. The text could be a letter or diary, or a piece of biography, autobiography or travel writing.

A **media text** is one that has its origins in the mass media – it could be a newspaper or magazine story, a piece from radio or television, or an advertising text.

2 Using fact and opinion

To begin with, this is fairly straightforward, but sorting out sensible definitions is always a worthwhile starting point.

A **fact** is a piece of information that can be confirmed. Below are a few basic examples:

Peter Murphy attends our school.

Spiders have eight legs.

It rained here yesterday.

She has blue eyes.

An **opinion** is an individual's view, interpretation or judgement. A few simple examples follow:

Netball is the best game there is!

'Coronation Street' is a wonderful programme.

He thinks he's just great.

Liverpool is the greatest team in the world.

ACTIVITY 1

Sort out the following statements – are they fact or opinion?

a   Shakespeare was a great playwright.

b   Shakespeare's plays are now a complete waste of space!

c   Martin Luther King was the greatest American of the twentieth century.

d   Martin Luther King was one of the most important figures in the American civil rights movement.

e   Large out-of-town supermarkets now provide 41% of us with our shopping needs.

f   Our traditional town centre shopping facilities are under threat from the giant out-of-town supermarkets.

g   There have been amazing advances in computing in the second half of the twentieth century.

h   Computers are the most important development in the second half of the twentieth century.

i   Mobile phones are nothing more than a designer accessory.

j   A mobile phone is useful in an emergency.

Look at the mixture of fact and opinion used in this paragraph.

I hate football! It's a terrible game. Twenty-two blokes all dressed in uniforms, running around after a ball trying to kick it. And for what reason? Only to try and put it in a big rectangle at the far end of a pitch. This is very strange behaviour!

FACT	OPINION
I hate football!	It's a terrible game.
Twenty-two blokes. . .kick it.	
to try and put it. . .at the far end of a pitch	
	This is very strange behaviour!

There should not have been any real difficulty in completing this task. But what is the effect of this change to the second sentence?

Twenty-two blokes all dressed in <u>silly</u> uniforms ..

It certainly alters things. The sentence is still factual in terms of the numbers playing and what they wear, but by describing their outfits as '*silly*' the writer colours the information with his/her own viewpoint.

Another observation before we leave this example: whilst we have analysed this paragraph in terms of fact and opinion, it certainly doesn't give us a complete picture of what is going on in this brief piece of writing.

Understanding the use made of fact and opinion tells us nothing of the deliberately mocking tone of the piece or the intentionally blunt and provocative approach of the writer. It also does not take into account the use of the rhetorical question which is designed to directly engage the reader.

To sort out the use an author has made of fact and opinion is to understand just one element that is to be found in the writer's bag of tricks.

The manipulation of fact and opinion

The colouring of fact and opinion is another technique that writers employ to further develop their viewpoint. Consider the following:

A worrying rise of 7% threatens to cause problems next year.

Note how the writer has referred to the rise of 7% using the adjective '*worrying*'. The reader is being told to be concerned and this concern is then heightened by the use of the phrase '*threatens to cause problems*'. The 7% increase – the fact at the heart of this statement – is being described in such a way as to colour the audience's view of it.

Here is an example of opinion being coloured:

Only someone with no dress sense at all would be prepared to be seen wearing one of these dreadful plastic anoraks.

The writer's opinion is that these plastic anoraks are awful. In order to drive home this viewpoint the writer employs a form of social blackmail. If the reader does not share his/her view that this is a 'dreadful' article of clothing, then the implication is that the individual has no taste whatsoever – a charge that would be likely to cause most of us to stop and think twice!

ACTIVITY 2

Here are some examples for you to assess. Sort out which are facts and which are opinions and then consider how the writers have attempted to manipulate the reader's outlook.

In a dramatic midnight raid, customs officials swooped to seize a shipment of drugs.

For the more discerning holidaymaker, the Caribbean is the only place to go.

Nurses are demanding a massive 40% pay rise and threatening to plunge our hospitals into chaos with a series of one-day strikes.

This car is so ugly, it's a wonder the manufacturers had the nerve to put their badge on it!

Stating opinion as fact

This is the technique where the writer states opinion in such a forceful manner that it may initially appear as if it were a fact. For example:

This is the best film ever made!

or

You are the worst dancer in the world!

One of the best-known examples of this technique is to be found in the opening sentence of Jane Austen's novel *Pride and Prejudice*:

It is a truth universally acknowledged, that a single man in possession of a good fortune, must be in want of a wife.

What Austen has done here is to present, in a playful and ironic manner, a view which is strongly held by some of the characters in her book. What gives the statement its humour is that it is clearly an opinion but it is presented as if it was a fact so obvious that it is indeed '*a truth universally acknowledged*'!

Fact and opinion at work

Below is the text taken from the opening page of a holiday brochure describing the attractions of Cyprus. Read it over carefully.

Cyprus may be a small country, but it's a large island — the third largest in the Mediterranean. And it's an island with a big heart — an island that gives its visitors a genuine welcome and treats them as friends.

With its spectacular scenery and enviable climate, it's no wonder that Aphrodite [the mythical Greek goddess of love] chose this island as her playground, and since then, mere mortals have been discovering this 'land fit for Gods' for themselves.

Cyprus is an island of beauty and a country of contrasts. Cool, pine-clad mountains are a complete scene-change after golden sun-kissed beaches; tranquil, timeless villages are in striking contrast to modern cosmopolitan towns; luxurious beachside hotels can be exchanged for large areas of natural, unspoilt countryside; yet in Cyprus all distances are easily manageable, mostly on modern roads and highways — with a secondary route or two for the more adventurous.

Most important of all, the island offers peace of mind. At a time when holidays are clouded by safety consciousness, a feeling of security prevails everywhere since the crime level is so low as to be practically non-existent.

What follows is a guided analysis of the use of fact and opinion in this piece of writing.

The writer's stance and purpose are relatively easy to grasp: to present a very positive and inviting view of the island to the audience who are potential holidaymakers.

Paragraph 1

The first sentence begins with a couple of contrasting and straightforward facts – *'a small country'* and *'a large island'*. The writer then completes the sentence with the further fact that the island of Cyprus is *'the third largest in the Mediterranean'*.

The next sentence, by contrast, consists solely of opinion. The island is said to have *'a big heart'*, which is reinforced by the opinion that it *'gives its visitors a genuine welcome and treats them as friends.'*

Paragraph 2

Here the use of opinion continues when the scenery is described as *'spectacular'* and the climate is *'enviable'*.

The attractive qualities of the island are further strengthened by the association between Aphrodite and the island. We are informed she chose it as *'her playground'*, and because of this association the writer is quick to describe the island as a *'land fit for Gods'*.

Paragraph 3

The *island–country* idea used in the first sentence of the text is employed again in the opening sentence of this paragraph. Opinion is presented as if it were fact – *'Cyprus is an island of beauty.'*

In a long and complex second sentence, the writer makes use of factual contrasts in order to support the very strongly stated opinion that is contained in the opening sentence. This also has the effect of adding to the all-round appeal of the island. The writer is creating images of a land of *'mountains'* and *'beaches'*, *'villages'* and *'towns'*, and *'hotels'* and *'countryside'*.

Look at the use that is made of pairs of adjectives to add detail and colour to manipulate the reader's response – the mountains are '*Cool pine-clad*'; the beaches are '*golden sun-kissed*'; the villages are '*tranquil, timeless*'; the towns are '*modern cosmopolitan*'; the hotels are '*luxurious beachside*' affairs; and the countryside is '*natural, unspoilt*'.

Paragraph 4

In the final paragraph the writer takes a different approach to the task of selling Cyprus to the reader. On this occasion the focus switches to '*safety*' and '*peace of mind*'.

Like the two preceding paragraphs this one again opens with a forceful statement that at first glance seems to be a fact but on closer inspection is the writer's opinion – '*Most important of all, the island offers peace of mind.*' What the writer actually means is, in his/her view, we should feel safe here, but that is not how it is expressed!

The very sensitive issue of safety is one we all share and by touching upon this and reassuring us that '*the crime level is so low as to be practically non-existent*', the writer is using a fact to conclude strongly and effectively.

ACTIVITY 3

Here you can see how this text was actually presented in the brochure. Consider how it tries to create an appropriate atmosphere to reinforce the messages in the text. Consider the effect of:

▸ the layout of the text on the page

▸ the use of the pictures

▸ the central image of Aphrodite.

3 Presenting information and developing a point of view

The article that follows is taken from a tabloid newspaper. The writer uses some factual material about body-piercing to present a very negative point of view about the subject.

You may disagree with the opinions expressed in this article. Resist the temptation to express your views on the subject of body-piercing – no matter how strongly you feel. Your personal thoughts and feelings are **not** required in this section of the examination and are **not** relevant.

The examiner, however, is interested in how well you can show your understanding of **how writers put across their views** to you, the reader.

So let's examine **how** the journalist Victoria Fletcher:

▸ presents information

▸ puts across her viewpoint

▸ develops her case against the issue.

It is important to realise that the writer of this article wants you, the reader, to share her viewpoint about the issue. She does this by **deliberately** using particular methods in order to develop her case and to influence you to share her point of view. These have been identified for you as follows:

The photographs

Naturally, our eyes are drawn to these right away. We are confronted with a row of three different photographs of 'deformed' ears. These are meant to provoke a response in the reader. The clear intention is to shock and horrify those who are browsing through the newspaper as well as to encourage them to read the article. It is also no accident that these are in close-up and are presented in colour. This has the effect of making them even more gruesome to look at. The pictures of 'cauliflower ears' revolt us and the writer has certainly succeeded in gaining our interest in the issue. Note the pointed remark underneath.

The larger photograph of an attractive young woman is intended to be a clear contrast to these. It, too, is in colour and in close-up. The subject is looking confidently into the camera with her pierced ear clearly in view. This is the desired look but underneath there is a dire warning that in attempting this, 'you could end up looking like a boxer'.

The headline and strapline

Both of these make it obvious what approach the article is going to take. The use of emotive words such as 'scourge' and 'scar you for life' send a clear message that the writer views the issue in a negative way. Notice how the headline is placed alongside the photograph of the young woman. This is so the reader doesn't miss the point that this practice can permanently deform ears.

Health experts seek body-piercing ban as 'cauliflower ear' scourge spreads

By Victoria Fletcher
Consumer Editor

THE NEW LOOK THAT COULD SCAR YOU FOR LIFE

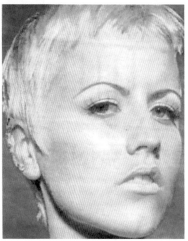

SO STYLISH: But you could end up looking like a boxer

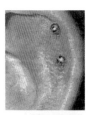

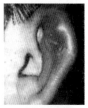

HIGH FASHION – and some of its less pleasing results

A new body-piercing trend is leaving young people disfigured for life.

Thousands of teenagers have grown large, misshapen 'cauliflower ears' after having them pierced at the top.

In just under ten years the number of people with cauliflower ears has doubled. Now more than 1,400 people have this worrying disorder, which experts link directly to beauty parlours' use of the wrong piercing equipment.

A report in the British Medical Journal urges doctors to look out for new piercings which could turn nasty. 'No official regulations exist on body-piercing,' it warns.

'Doctors should be on the lookout for this dangerous condition as early involvement helps to prevent the serious consequences that can occur in young people who have under-gone high-ear piercing.'

Specialists believe that piercing 'guns' are wrongly used on the top part of the ear. These crush the cartilage, causing the deformity.

'This equipment is not appropriate for cutting through cartilage because it leaves it open and gets it infected,' said Dr Stephen Kent, an ear, nose and throat consultant at Warrington Hospital. 'Most people performing this practice do not appear to be aware of the dangers. It is quite appalling. Customers should be warned that they might end up with scarring.'

The British Medical Journal report comes only days after an official report, published by The Chartered Institute of Environmental Health, warned that extra care must be taken with the top of the ear. 'A piercing there will take up to a year to heal, compared with just weeks for the ear lobe.'

In fact, so concerned is the CIEH about the many problems caused by body-piercing, that it calls for piercings below the neck – such as the tummy piercing sported by so many pop stars – to be made illegal for under-16's.

You have been warned!

From an article by Victoria Fletcher in the *Sunday Express*, 26 August 2001

Use of 'expert' opinion

The first words of the strapline are 'Health experts' and the writer sprinkles her article with references such as the 'British Medical Journal', 'specialists' and 'The Chartered Institute of Environmental Health'. She uses quotes from two important sounding reports to help build up her case. For example we are told that 'No official regulations exist' and that piercing at the top of the ear 'will take up to a year to heal'.

In addition, the writer uses a lengthy quote from a Dr Stephen Kent who is a hospital consultant – a 'specialist'. We learn that piercing equipment is often 'wrongly used' and can 'crush the cartilage'. He feels the situation is 'quite appalling' and that 'Customers should be warned'.

This all adds weight to the writer's negative stance as these experts convey the impression that they know what they are talking about and that their opinions can be trusted. Victoria Fletcher has the experts on her side so she must be right – this is the perception being created.

Making words work

The article opens with a sweeping statement that overstates the situation. It makes it out to be more serious than it actually is, but does provide a dramatic opening to the article.

This is followed by a further factual-sounding statement about the 'Thousands of teenagers' afflicted with 'cauliflower ears'. This point is supported in the next paragraph by what appears to be statistical evidence – how in 'under ten years' the figure 'has doubled' to 'more than 1,400 people'. Whether or not this information is factual is open to debate – the references to 'Thousands of teenagers' and 'more than 1,400 people' don't match up for example. However, the way it is being presented, using a confident tone, is very convincing to read.

Adjectives are used in the first few paragraphs to create a sense of alarm and to key the reader in to the enormity of the problem. The writer wants to generate feelings of worry and concern so she refers to '**misshapen** "cauliflower ears"', '**serious** consequences', 'this **dangerous** condition' and 'this **worrying** disorder'. Using this slant helps persuade the audience to share her particular standpoint.

Even though it isn't directly relevant, the writer devotes a whole paragraph to the call for banning tummy piercing for under-sixteens. This is to add emphasis to her case and to highlight the serious nature of body-piercing in general.

Another clever way to involve the audience in the debate is the use of the word 'you'. There are several examples of this device in the article. This method of speaking directly to the reader is very persuasive and is how the writer chooses to finish off the article: 'You have been warned!' This is a suitably short and snappy concluding sentence which is intended to leave the audience in no doubt as to the significance of the problem.

4 Structuring writing and methods of presentation

How a piece of written material is **structured** directly relates to how a writer has **organised his/her ideas** on a subject or issue. The structure, therefore, helps a writer achieve **his/her purpose**.

Presentational devices such as pictures, layout and use of colour also have an important role to play in **emphasising** the main message to the reader.

Let's examine how this is achieved in the newspaper article 'Child's Play'. This article has a clear structure or **shape** that leads the reader, step by step, through the writer's views on the subject of American wrestling. Presentational devices have also been employed to reinforce these views.

The reader's attention will always caught by the picture and the headline. Writers are aware of this and considerable care is taken over the headline, its size and positioning in relation to the picture.

Let's look and see how this writer has dealt with these two presentational devices.

The headline – 'Child's Play'

A headline usually makes clear the writer's stance on a topic. In this case the play on words is intriguing but what makes the point that wrestling is not being viewed as an innocent activity is the way that the **headline** and the **picture** have been deliberately placed **side by side**.

There is also a link between the headline and the summary beside it. A sense of unease is communicated through the question posed at the end of the summary. Note how the use of alliteration helps to strengthen the notion that there is a problem.

All of this leaves the reader in no doubt that the writer of this article takes a negative stance towards this issue.

The pictures

The **photograph** of two boys watching a wrestling match on television is intended to worry parents. What they are watching is violent and the very large screen appears to dominate the two boys so that they look quite vulnerable. This striking image also dominates the article, perhaps to convey the impression that wrestlers are larger-than-life characters.

The Fight Club is another presentational device. The photographs are meant to look like a rogues' gallery and support the view presented in the article that the wrestlers are 'unsavoury weirdos'. The lurid details are intended to support this view as well as to provoke outrage and distaste in the reader.

The structure of the article

Section 1

The first four paragraphs focus on the Rock. The purpose of the opening paragraph is to create, in a dramatic way, an impression of his popularity. This is built upon in the following three paragraphs with lots of factual information to establish his status as a superstar.

These facts, along with some emotive language such as 'more worryingly' and 'He has come for your children', are meant to engender fear and concern in parents about the suitability of the Rock as a role model.

Section 2

The next three paragraphs present even more factual information but this time to establish the popularity of US wrestling with children. The reader is bombarded with all these facts to highlight the view that this is a 'phenomenon' that is 'gripping young people'. The section finishes by posing a question regarding whether or not this sport generates a threat to children.

Section 3

The question as to whether or not this sport poses a threat to children is answered in the next seven paragraphs of the article as the writer considers the case against wrestling.

CHILD'S PLAY

Brash, brutal and bigger than live football – US wrestlers have become the new role models for many youngsters in Britain. Should we be worried, asks Rosie Waterhouse?

The music hits you first, with its anthem: 'Do you smell what the Rock is cooking?' More than 20,000 people inside London's Earls Court leap to attention as a 6ft 5in tall, muscle-bound figure splits the stage curtains and enters to a blinding show of strobe lighting. Another quarter of a million are watching at home on television.

The Rock is Dwayne Johnson, a graduate from the University of Miami with top marks for speech communication who now styles himself the 'most electrifying man in sports entertainment'. He has come for your children.

The Rock is a 27-year-old American wrestler. He is also a best-selling author, a pin-up in Britain's biggest-selling calendar and the face on more T-shirts than any pop star you could care to name.

Your children can buy the Rock's music on CD, his picture for a new sticker book and, more worryingly, his fighting skills on a computer game that sold 68,000 copies in its first week.

Tickets for these wrestling extravaganzas sell for up to £30 with shows grossing up to £2m. The pre-teenage children who make up most of the audiences spend on average £15 each on merchandising – three times the takings at a pop concert.

Wrestling now attracts a bigger audience than live premiership soccer, apart from those games featuring Manchester United. It is Channel 4's top-rated sports programme, with up to 2m viewers and has six of the top 10 best-selling sports videos in Britain.

It is a phenomenon that has not only taken America by storm but is also gripping young people, primarily aged eight to fourteen. What is its appeal and should parents be worried by its diet of violence and swearing?

Mick McManus, a wrestling hero in the 1960s and 1970s, admits the

Americans have got televised wrestling 'down to a fine art' but that it's all 'harmless fun'.

'Kids nowadays are hooked on superheroes and monsters in comics and videos, and the new-style wrestling is really just an extension of that. It's as if these strange characters have walked off the page into the ring,' he said. Unlike in McManus's day, there is no pretence that it is a competitive sport. Everyone knows the bouts are fixed, with the wrestlers rehearsing their moves beforehand. In fact it is more like some sort of athletic soap opera as scriptwriters are often brought in to work on character and plots with the wrestlers. This is packaged as 'entertainment' but is simply a thin excuse to parade unsavoury weirdos engaged in violent, staged bust-ups.

Oliver Sterling, a 12-year-old fan from Essex, said: 'My mum thinks WWF is dreadful, but I just think it's great fun. Dad doesn't mind too much because he knows I realise the results are fixed and the falls are not as bad as they appear.'

In defence of WWF the Rock has stated: 'The violence in the ring is of the comic-book, action-adventure variety. And everybody comes back to fight another day.'

Wrong! Wrestlers suffer broken bones, second degree burns, concussion and even worse. Mick Foley had one of his ears ripped off when a manoeuvre on the ropes, known as the Hangman, went wrong. Many schools across the country have banned children from

STONE COLD STEVE AUSTIN
Also known as the Texas Rattlesnake, the 35-year-old's trademark is drinking beer in the ring. Famous for giving one-fingered signs to the crowd.

MICK FOLEY, ALIAS MANKIND
He once had an ear ripped off during a bout. Takes part in Japanese death matches in which barbed wire replaces the ring ropes.

CHYNA
Billed as the ninth wonder of the world and the first woman to compete in the Royal Rumble, a premier annual wrestling event. "I'm telling women 'it's okay to be different'," she says

DAVY 'BOY' SMITH
Alias the British Bulldog. The most successful British WWF fighter. Married to the sister of Owen Hart, a wrestler who died in the ring last year.

THE ROCK
Also known as the People's Champion. Real name Dwayne Johnson. Author of The Rock Says. Both his father and grandfather were wrestlers. Previously fought under the names of Flex Kavana and Rocky Maivia. Favourite phrase: every opponent is 'a candyass jabroni'

MAE YOUNG
Now in her late seventies. A former female wrestling superstar, she returned to the ring last year. Last weekend she threw a bucket of water over an opponent at London's Earl's Court.

Pictures: World Wrestling Federation

restaging WWF bouts in the playground after a 6-year-old girl in America was killed by a friend who was imitating one of the Rock's moves, which he had seen on television.

Sky Television now broadcasts a 'don't try this at home' warning before wrestling events but wrestler Darren Matthews will still not allow his own children to watch.

Harmless fun? I don't think so!

From an article by Rosie Waterhouse in *The Sunday Times*, 14 May 2000

ACTIVITY 4

You need to be able to **identify** arguments being presented and comment on **how writers use evidence** to support their viewpoints. Read Section 3 of the article and:

▸ identify the arguments offered

▸ consider the supporting evidence used

▸ assess the effectiveness of the arguments and the evidence.

Section 4

The article ends with a strong statement to conclude the case against US wrestling. The fact that a fighter won't let his own children watch a match allows the writer to finish off her article with an emphatic flourish: 'Harmless fun? I don't think so!' There is also a strong sarcastic tone to this final remark which emphasises the writer's fierce disapproval.

The role of presentational devices

Presentational devices are used most extensively in brochures and leaflets. It is to these that we are now going to look. Before we begin it is important to understand the role of **presentational** devices. They assist in:

▸ fulfilling the **purpose** of a text

▸ appealing to the **audience** for which a text is intended.

Presentational devices combine together to **enhance the appearance** of texts and to **maximise the impact** with the target audience. Presentational devices you are most likely to encounter are:

▸ use of colour

▸ use of visual images

▸ headings and subheadings

▸ layout of text

▸ use of different font styles and sizes.

You need to be able to **identify** what devices are being used, **comment** on their effectiveness in achieving the writer's purpose and **analyse** how they add to the overall appeal of a text.

The use of presentational devices

In order to study these presentational devices, we are going to consider how they work in a leaflet for an aquarium called Exploris. On the right is the front page.

In terms of **purpose**, this leaflet is essentially an advertisement so it sets out to persuade potential customers to visit the Exploris aquarium. It is also written to inform readers

EXPLORIS
the northern ireland aquarium

open daily

as close as you can get without getting wet!

EXPLORIS aquarium

is Northern Ireland's only aquarium and seal sanctuary. It is an award winning visitor facility and one of the country's must see attractions. Exploris is located in the conservation village of Portaferry, on the shores of Strangford Lough, one of the most important marine sites in Europe.

Exploris is the perfect venue for an exciting day out for all ages.

Touch Tanks
A chance for you to touch and hold a variety of living marine animals. Stroke a friendly ray. Feel the suction power of a spiny starfish. Tickle a prickly sea urchin. Exploris' touch tanks are run by experienced guides at regular intervals throughout each day.

Feeding time
Experience the frenzy of feeding time at Exploris - seals or fish may be being fed at the time of your visit - ask at reception for details.

Open Sea Tank
Our huge Open Sea Tank, recently remodelled, holds more than a quarter of a million litres of water, as well as lots of interesting fish life. Gaze into deep waters, where sharks circle and rays sweep majestically past. It is as close as you can get without a wetsuit!

Marine Discovery Lab
Take a closer look at marine life in our new lab, complete with it's own mini touch tank. The animals here are always changing - from delicate fish embryos to a microscopic world under the video microscope.

New displays
Exploris has made some major changes to it's displays of fish and marine life. There are several new tanks including a special jellyfish display. Come and see for yourself the changes that we have made since your last visit.

What other facilities can we offer you?
Gift shop : Cafe : Park and picnic area
Children's playground : Caravan park : Woodland
Bowling green : Parent and baby room

Group bookings
Exploris Aquarium runs an education service, offering excellent tours for groups, featuring live animals and fun activities, led by experienced staff. Exploris provides groups with a stimulating learning experience or simply a fun day out - you choose.

Wolfie Club for kids
This is a fun club aimed at the under 12s, where kids can find out more about sea life. By joining the Wolfie Club, children receive their own newsletter along with details about special events and competitions.

Birthday parties
From September through to March, children can hold their birthday parties at Exploris. These are suitable for all ages, and include a guided tour, goody bags, party food, and special activities.

Friends of Exploris
Any visitor can become a special Friend of Exploris by purchasing an annual ticket at reception. This offers an unlimited number of visits throughout the year, as well as regular updates on events and activities.

New features

NIE Seal Sanctuary
This new facility was opened in 2000, and is home to Northern Ireland's sick or orphaned seal pups. Every year Exploris rehabilitates these abandoned pups and gets them ready to return to the wild.

The NIE Seal Sanctuary takes you through the seals' journey back to health - from the pens where the pups are kept when they are very young, right through to the ponds where they learn to swim. There are special viewing points for visitors to see the seals - from above, alongside and underwater.

Returning to the wild
Exploris rehabilitates the sick or injured seals. This means that when the seals are ready, they are released back into the wild. At certain times of the year Exploris is more likely to have a number of seal pups in residence. This is because both grey and common seals give birth to pups two times in the year. If you are particularly interested in viewing the seals, please call ahead for more information about their availability.

Opening Times

	April - Aug	Sept - March
Mon - Fri	10am - 6pm	10am - 5pm
Sat	11am - 6pm	11am - 5pm
Sun	1pm - 6pm	1pm - 5pm

By road
From Belfast take the A20 through Newtownards and on to Portaferry.

Where are we?

By ferry
Take the A25 from Downpatrick to Strangford. Follow signs to the Strangford ferry - the journey to Portaferry across the Lough takes less than 15 minutes. For timetable information on the Strangford Ferry, telephone 028 4488 1637.

On arrival in Portaferry, Exploris is signposted and easy to find.

Contact us

EXPLORIS aquarium

Exploris Aquarium, The Rope Walk, Castle Street, Portaferry, Co. Down, Northern Ireland BT22 1NZ

Tel: 028 4272 8062 Fax: 028 4272 8396
e-mail: info@exploris.org.uk
web site: www.exploris.org.uk

about the facilities on offer. In terms of **audience**, it is aimed at families with children, animal lovers and the environmentally aware.

What follows is an analysis of the presentational devices used in the leaflet.

Use of colour

The colours used in this leaflet make it eye-catching and visually very attractive. The dominant background colours of turquoise, green and blue have been carefully chosen as appropriate for a leaflet with an aquatic theme. In fact, these marine colours are meant to convey the sensation of being 'underwater' in one of the tanks.

Brightly coloured sea creatures on the front page and inside the leaflet add further interest and highlight particularly interesting sea life that can be encountered at the aquarium.

Use of visual images

These mainly set out to communicate the impression that there are many exciting things to do at Exploris so that any visitor is guaranteed a stimulating and fun-filled day out. Close-up photographs of a variety of marine life and selected demonstrations give an indication of the range of displays and activities available.

The interactive nature of these activities is also being reinforced through the photographs of children holding marine animals and looking happily absorbed as they increase their knowledge about sea life. The message is clear – these children are having a wonderful and educational experience, learning all about these fascinating creatures.

The appeal of this visitor attraction to children is further reinforced by the appearance of the cartoon character Wolfie the wolf fish to advertise the special Wolfie Club, and the picture of NIEL the seal, Exploris's new mascot.

There is also a useful map of Northern Ireland at the back of the leaflet showing visitors where Exploris is situated.

Headings and subheadings

The Exploris logo is used as a heading on the front of the leaflet and again inside. Such repetition is a common device to familiarise the reader with a brand name or logo.

The subheadings are used to draw the reader's attention to the main highlights of the facilities Exploris has to offer, as they guide the reader's eye through the main body of the leaflet. The large number of these subheadings is intended to give the sense that there is a wide variety of stimulating activities available.

Note that these subheadings are boxed and are coloured alternatively blue or green to add more visual impact. One subheading poses a question in an attempt to directly involve the reader.

Layout of text

Notice how the words and phrases in this leaflet are laid out in manageable 'chunks' or sections under each subheading. Breaking up the text in this way has the effect of making the information about all that is available at this visitor centre more accessible and easier for the reader to absorb.

Straightforward instructions regarding how to contact Exploris and how to get there are set out clearly and simply on the back page. Opening times are laid out in table form – again making this vital information readily available for the reader .

Use of different font styles and sizes

The Exploris logo has been given its own individual touch through the use of distinctive flourishes in the lettering. Particularly noticeable is the use of a swirl for the 'O', which echoes the appearance of an ammonite. This swirl is subtly featured in several corners of the leaflet – again adding to the overall visual appeal.

As would normally be expected, the text in the subheadings has a larger font than that used for the information underneath each of these. It is important that even a casual browser, who only looks at the photographs and subheadings, will absorb the main aspects of what's on offer at Exploris.

The role of language

It is equally important to understand the role of **language** in helping to:

▷ fulfil the **purpose** of a text
▷ appeal to the **audience** for which a text is intended.

The language used will **match** the purpose and intended audience of a text. This is an important means of manipulating the reader's response and, as with presentational devices, you have to be able to **identify** the devices a writer has used and **comment** on how these are meant to affect the target audience.

The use of language

Having considered the impact made by the appearance of the Exploris leaflet, we now need to do the same with the words and phrases used to engage the reader's interest and to persuade the reader to consider a visit to Exploris.

What follows is a breakdown of the use of language – or linguistic devices – in the leaflet.

▷ The tone of the leaflet is friendly and there is a sense of enthusiasm about the facilities available. This is conveyed in language like, 'as close as you can get without getting wet!' The use of rhyme along with the exclamation mark increases the impression of pleasantness and helpfulness along with a sense of fun.

▷ The introductory section uses positive vocabulary that sets out to establish Exploris as a well regarded and reputable visitor centre. These phrases help relay this viewpoint: 'Northern Ireland's **only** aquarium and seal sanctuary', '**award winning** visitor facility', 'located in one of the **most important** marine sites in Europe'.

▷ Use of flattering adjectives increases the reader's confidence and interest in what Exploris has to offer visitors. Look at these examples: 'the **perfect** venue', 'an **exciting** day out', '**excellent** tours', '**experienced** staff', '**special** events', 'an **unlimited** number'.

▷ The language chosen to present information about the main attractions conveys a sense of fun and excitement. For example, the reader is informed that there is an 'Open Sea Tank … where sharks circle and rays sweep majestically past'.

▷ Factual details are used to impress. Thus, the Open Sea Tank has been 'recently remodelled' and 'holds more than a quarter of a million litres of water'.

▷ The reader is addressed individually. Under the subheading 'Touch Tanks' we read: 'A chance for **you** to touch and hold a variety of living marine animals' along with examples likely to be encountered such as 'a spiny starfish' and 'a prickly sea urchin'.

▶ Use is made of imperatives – special words that give the reader instructions. Requests to '**Experience** the frenzy of feeding', '**Come and see** for yourself', '**Take** a closer look', and '**Feel** the suction power' have the effect of inviting the reader to pay a visit to Exploris and tempting them to participate in these exciting activities.

▶ Use is made of details which suggest that a trip to Exploris would be of special interest to families with children. Hence, the opportunity to touch and hold the marine life is referred to several times; using 'the video microscope' would also have family appeal. Likewise, references to the 'Children's playground', the 'Wolfie Club' and 'birthday parties' would all engage the interest of parents and children.

▶ The vocabulary chosen conveys the impression that a visit to Exploris would have educational value. For example, the reader is told that there is a 'Marine Discovery Lab' and that 'Exploris provides groups with a stimulating learning experience'.

▶ The vocabulary selected suggests that Exploris is an environmentally friendly organization. For instance, the reader is informed that Exploris 'is located in the conservation village of Portaferry', 'home to Northern Ireland's sick or orphaned seal pups', 'rehabilitates these abandoned pups' and 'gets them ready to return to the wild'.

▶ The vocabulary used reassures the reader that Exploris is constantly updating its facilities. The writer is keen to point out that the Open Sea Tank has been 'recently remodelled', that there is a 'new' Marine Discovery Lab with animals that are 'always changing' and that there have been some 'major changes to its displays. . .including a special jellyfish display' .

▶ Special offers such as group bookings and joining 'Friends of Exploris' are highlighted as these can be ways for potential visitors to save money.

ACTIVITY 5

Here is another leaflet. Again, the front page, the three-segment centre spread and the two-segment back pages are shown. Study the leaflet carefully and answer these questions.

a   What is the leaflet's purpose and intended audience?

b   How does the writer use presentational devices?

c   How has language been used to put the leaflet's message across?

Keeping Smart Online !

See if you can remember these 5 Safety Tips, and then prove to your friends and parents that you are a SMART surfer.

SECRET – Always keep your name, address, mobile phone number and password private - it's like giving out the keys to your home !

MEETING someone you have contacted in cyberspace can be dangerous. Only do so with your parent's/carer's permission, and then when they can be present.

ACCEPTING e-mails or opening files from people you don't really know or trust can get you into trouble - they may contain viruses or nasty messages.

REMEMBER someone online may be lying and not be who they say they are. Stick to the public areas in chat rooms and if you feel uncomfortable simply get out of there !

TELL your parent or carer if someone or something makes you feel uncomfortable or worried.

"The Internet is a great tool and we use it to keep in touch with our fans. However, it is really important that we all learn to use the Net safely and we would encourage all young people in Northern Ireland to learn these SMART rules and stay safe online"

Six.

Need Further Advice ?

If things get out of hand online or you need to talk to someone about something you've seen or someone you've been talking to online, you should talk to a sympathetic teacher at school, or your parents or carers. You can also talk to a counsellor on:

NSPCC Child Protection Helpline:
email: help@nspcc.org.uk
Freephone: 0808 800 5000
Textphone: 0800 560566

ChildLine 24-hour Helpline:
Freephone: 0800 1111
Web: www.childline.org.uk

or contact your local Social Services

See also these websites for great advice:

www.nch.org.uk/itok/   www.chatdanger.com
www.kidsmart.org.uk   www.thinkuknow.co.uk
www.there4me.com

This leaflet has been produced by the Northern Ireland Area Child Protection Committees.

To order further copies ring 028 37 414614

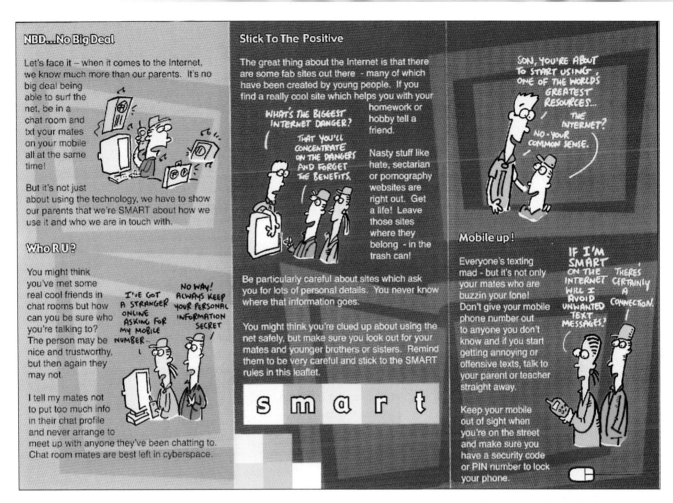

5 Using words and phrases

The last piece of work on leaflets, which increasingly focused on language, makes clear the degree of overlap that is present within the four subsections that have been created in order to study the writer's craft. It is unwise to think that words and phrases in isolation can give us a complete picture. Bearing this in mind, we will move on to the next text.

This is an article by a newspaper columnist who writes regularly for a paper. (In such articles the columnist is usually developing his/her own personal opinions on an important subject of the day. As a result, such articles tend to consist largely of opinion although they may contain a few facts.)

In this text the writer is presenting his rather unusual personal views about the involvement of the England football team in the World Cup 2002.

A word of warning! When analysing and responding to a text such as this, avoid being drawn into developing your own views on the topic. As we are focusing on use of language, your task is to identify and comment on the approaches to language that have been used by a writer. You are required to comment on the writer's language skills, **not** on the issue they are dealing with.

Now read the article and the guided commentary that follows.

Why I can't wait for it to be all over for England

I hope the English football team is rapidly knocked out of the World Cup! I really do!

And please don't call this group of people 'England'. They are not England and do not represent this country, at least I sincerely hope they don't. They are people who happen to be fairly good at playing football and who happen to be English.

An early defeat would silence all those unhinged, half-hysterical voices jabbering on about victory and defeat.

Honestly, what difference would it make if 'we' won? Would we be more or less free? Would we be more prosperous? More or less safe from war? More or less better edu-cated? None of the above.

It would make precisely no differ-ence. It doesn't matter. I suspect there is a huge minority who either actively loathe this ugly game, which seems to attract violence and drunkenness as a dirty dustbin attracts bluebottles, or are bored to screaming point by it.

We don't like the sly cheating, the faked agony, the absurd over-dramatisation of 22 men kicking a bladder about between two sets of sticks and string.

We don't like the foul-mouthed chants or the mobs of fat, beery men clad in football strip, who could barely run 20 yards without risking cardiac arrest.

But, above all, we don't like the arrogant assumption that this is the most important thing in the world. I quite like playing football, but I wouldn't want to watch it. I quite like bricklaying too, but I wouldn't want to watch someone else doing it for 90 minutes. We soccer refuseniks [people not interested in football] are tolerant. We have no objection to other people watching this stuff or talking about it until they fall asleep in the nearest puddle of lager.

But we don't see why it should be assumed that the rest of us care when we don't. We don't see why our entire culture should be taken over for weeks by this non-event.

So because ... I have had just enough of people who have no sense of what matters and what dosen't, I long for 'us' to lose.

From an article by Peter Hitchens in the *Mail on Sunday*, 2 June 2002

Having read the article, let's consider:

▶ the writer's **purpose**

▶ the **tone** of the text

▶ the use of **language**.

The writer's purpose

He obviously has very negative views about football and wants to persuade his readers to share these views. One of his purposes, therefore, is to manipulate the readers' view. As a newspaper columnist his job is to entertain, to arouse and to sustain the interest of his reader. Thus, he has composed here an article that is lively, engaging and controversial.

The tone of the text

The tone of a piece of writing often conveys the writer's attitude towards his/her subject. The tone is conveyed through the type of language he/she frequently uses. Here, the writer seems to despise football – his tone is very negative and cynical. Thus the text is full of words of contempt for the game of football; for example, he calls it an *"ugly game"*.

The use of language

The following is a breakdown of the language – or linguistic devices – used by the writer to engage the interest of his readers:

▶ a striking **headline** – the unusual opinion that he *'can't wait'* for the England team to be defeated

▶ use of **repetition** (and an exclamation mark) in the first paragraph to reinforce his controversial view – *'I really do!'*

▶ a **wide range of critical opinions** about football:

● **the players** – they are only *'fairly good* at playing football'

● **the commentators** – the expression *'jabbering on'* implies that they are talking nonsense

● **the game itself** – he belittles the game by referring to it as just *'kicking a bladder about between two sets of sticks and string'* and suggests it consists of *'sly cheating'* and *'faked agony'*

● **the fans** – his attack on them is particularly scathing – he describes them as *'mobs of fat, beery men, clad in football strip'* who are only interested in *'violence and drunkenness'*

▶ use of **sarcastic tone** – he mocks the hype – *'those unhinged, half-hysterical voices jabbering'* and pokes fun at the fans' discussions – *'until they fall asleep in the nearest puddle of lager'*

▶ use of **rhetorical questions** (these are questions that have only one, obvious answer) – *'Would we be more or less free?'* Four of these are used in a list to make the writer's point even more forcefully when he finally presents the obvious answer: *'None of the above.'*

▶ use of an unpleasant **simile** to illustrate his cynical view of football as a game – it attracts *'violence and drunkenness as a dirty dustbin attracts bluebottles'* (the game is like a dirty dustbin and the *'bluebottles'* are, of course, the fans!)

▶ use of highly critical **adjectives** to describe football and the World Cup competition – *'sly'*, *'absurd'* and *'ugly'*

▶ use of **humour**, again of a sarcastic nature – his comparison of football with *'bricklaying'*

▶ occasional use of **alliteration** to enliven his language – *'dirty dustbin'*

▶ a **pretence at being fair** – he claims that he is *'tolerant'* of others and their opinions, but by the end of the same sentence he is blatantly unfair, suggesting that football fans bore themselves to sleep *'in the nearest puddle of lager'*

▸ **apparent use of facts** to back up his views, but the 'facts' are unconvincing – he only has reason to *'suspect'* there is a huge minority who are against football

▸ use of '**we**' (rather than 'I') to suggest that many people, including his readers, share his personal views – *'We don't like the foul-mouthed chants'*

▸ a **challenging** ending to his article – he explains that his patience has run out, he has *'had just enough'*. In order to teach people a lesson as to what really is important in life he wants to see England lose. (Note the sarcastic use of 'us' at the very end of the piece – he has spent most of his article making it clear that he has nothing in common with English football supporters!)

Answering effectively

In this passage the writer may be presenting views with which many readers would not agree, but he is undoubtedly a very clever writer who is skilled in the use of language. Remember, your task is to identify and comment on those skills, not to present your own views on the subject.

When commenting on the writer's use of language, remember that you need to quote examples to back up the points you are making. The suggested comments above show you how to make use of quotations and how to add them into your commentary.

ACTIVITY 6

Read the passage again. See if you can identify any other clever tricks of language used by this writer.

ACTIVITY 7

Now let's apply these skills to a non-fiction text. *The following account is from a book by travel writer Pete McCarthy about his experiences on a flight from England to Gibraltar.*

It's frosty and still dark as we board the plane at a ghastly shopping mall with an overcrowded airport attached, somewhere in Sussex. The young man in the seat next to me is Estonian, like his friend across the aisle. When breakfast is served he orders two quarter-bottles of red wine from a surprised stewardess and knocks them back at high speed with his sausage, bacon, mushrooms and powdered egg. Then he eats his muesli and yoghurt. It's so early my brain isn't working properly and I'm struggling to decipher [understand] the meaning of such extreme behaviour.   5

The Estonians are accompanied by a hearty English business type in a Winnie-the-Pooh-on-a-balloon tie who is keen to show that he's in charge. He keeps telling the Estonians very boring things in a loud, slow voice, leaving out all the definite and indefinite articles [every 'a' and 'the'], like a whisky trader talking to Injuns about the heap powerful thundersticks. When the   10
stewardess comes to collect the breakfast debris, my Estonian orders gin and tonic to wash the wine down, while his friend chooses a cup of tea and some port. I have been to Estonia twice and can report that it is indeed an enigmatic [strange] country.

We're crossing southern Spain when the pilot announces on the intercom that the weather isn't very nice in Gibraltar. Very windy, apparently. More than fifty miles per hour.   15

'Under the circumstances it would be hazardous to attempt a landing. We'll get back to you in a few minutes to let you know what's happening.'

'WINDY!' shouts Winnie-the-Pooh at the Estonians. 'NOT LANDING! DANGEROUS! GO! SOMEWHERE ELSE!'

He's using his right hand to mime what he thinks is a change of direction, but the Estonians   20 think is a plane crash. They have taken on the haunted look of men who are about to plummet from 36,000 feet and don't know whether to use their last seconds to proposition the stewardess or order more gin and port.

Before they can decide, we enter a cloud and the plane starts pitching and bumping in the most terrifying manner. It feels as if the controls have been seized by two teenage boys who   25 are pulling and pushing everything to see who can make a wing fall off first. Clouds look such gentle, fluffy things, so what's inside them that can cause aircraft such grief? Monsters? A giant anvil? Gods who are displeased with us? Not for the first time I find myself wondering whether you remain conscious and have a brilliant but eye-watering view all the way to the ground, or to the sharks.   30

We ricochet wildly down through the clouds and suddenly we're clear of them, descending rapidly but seemingly still in control. The PA system bing-bongs and the pilot is back on the airwaves. 'We've decided we'll try and give it a go anyway.'

His voice is alarmingly casual. I suppose he's trying to reassure us, but his words couldn't be more worrying if they'd been spoken in a drunken slur . . . We're now very close to something   35 that looks like the sea. I can see white tops on the waves. I can see individual drops of water, but no sign of land anywhere as we go into an abrupt gung-ho bank to the right that suggests our man is a frustrated fighter pilot . . . All around me passengers are exchanging panic-stricken glances with complete strangers with whom they've so far been scrupulously avoiding any kind of eye contact.   40

And now there it is in front of us, the Rock [of Gibraltar] itself, massive, grey, broody, windswept; but, above all, very solid-looking. The PA pings back on.

'I'm afraid this may be a little bumpy.' And that's it. He's gone quiet. Perhaps one of the stewards has managed to force a towel into his mouth before he could add, 'but I really couldn't give a toss.' We're hurtling flat and low across the water, straight towards the Rock. Why are we   45 so low? To get below the radar? Are we going to bomb it? We're so low over the spray that I can feel it on my face; or is that just the Estonians crying? And now there's the airstrip straight ahead of us, immediately beneath the enormous bulk of the Rock. At such close range it really does look dauntingly dense. If we do hit it, it is unlikely we'll have the option of surviving for at least ten days by eating each other.   50

A brutal gust of wind strikes the plane, tipping the wing on my side up towards the Rock, then down towards the seabed. We take another belt, then another, and now it's rolling crazily, feeling as if we're about to flip over like one of those eejits who fly upside down over Biggin Hill [an airfield] for charity on Bank Holiday Monday. We're dropping ever lower, rolling from side to side in newer and scarier ways, when without warning . . . we surge into   55 a steep, last-minute climb away from disaster. I can see people in Gibraltar going to work in their cars and thinking, 'What in God's name was that?' But they're disappearing rapidly into the distance as we climb back to a safe, or possibly unsafe height. Confident that he's given the Red Baron [a famous German fighter pilot from the First World War] the slip, our

man is back on the PA, sounding strangely low-key and matter-of-fact. 60

'Well, as you can see we were unable to land at Gibraltar. We'll keep you posted.'

Ten minutes later, we're dropping down over calm seas and miles and miles of . . . deserted sandy beach to land in Tangier, which is where I want to be tomorrow, but not today. 65

From *The Road to McCarthy* by Pete McCarthy

The writer's purpose is to entertain/amuse his readers with his account of a nightmare flight. Think about how the writer sustains the reader's interest.

Then answer the following questions. They are intended to help you bring together the analytical skills you have learnt and apply them to a text.

a What tense is the writer using? How does this assist him as he describes the events?

b Is the writer's style formal or informal? Use evidence to support your conclusion.

c How does the writer describe the airport in lines 1–2? What is curious about this description?

d What is the effect upon the reader of the description of his fellow passengers' unusual breakfast?

e The second paragraph contains a description of the Englishman accompanying the two Estonians. How does the writer create a humorous picture of this man?

f Look again at lines 16–22. Why is this humorous?

g What words on lines 18–19 has the writer used to add to the sense of unease?

h Consider the writer's description of the motion of the plane in lines 21–23.

i Look at the writer's use of internal monologue in lines 23–26. Can you identify where this technique is used elsewhere in the text?

j Consider the contrast between the conditions and the pilot's voice in lines 27–31.

k How has the writer built up the tension as they attempt to land at Gibraltar? Consider:
   ▸ the description of the movement of the plane
   ▸ the reactions of his fellow passengers
   ▸ the appearance of the Rock itself
   ▸ his thoughts about the pilot's remarks
   ▸ the use of humorous questions
   ▸ the description of the plane's final approach
   ▸ his thoughts about what the residents of Gibraltar are thinking
   ▸ the tone of the final comments of the pilot on the PA.

How to approach media and non-fiction: a summary

The simple flow chart that follows is an attempt to condense, on to a single page, all the steps and techniques that have been demonstrated and discussed in this section of the book. Its purpose is to give you an overview of how you can methodically work through analysing these types of texts.

Analysing non-fiction and media texts

1 Assess the writer's purpose, stance, tone and audience

Ask yourself whether the writer is attempting:
* to support or promote a particular view
* to present a balanced discussion
* to influence the reader's view
* to respond to views expressed in another document
* to provoke, entertain, educate, flatter, belittle or raise concerns.

What can you learn from the tone of the writing? Is it negative, positive, flattering, mocking, enthusiastic, angry or apportioning blame?

By sorting out the answers to these questions you will clarify what the writer is trying to achieve in the writing.

Does the writer have a specific audience in mind, such as parents, young people, pet owners, shoppers, the unemployed or potential holidaymakers?

4 Think about the use made of style as well as language (words and phrases) to develop a point of view

Of course this is an artificial division because the majority of what has gone before is carried through words and phrases.

Look out for the use made of:
* standard and colloquial English
* emotive language
* direct appeals to the reader – 'I' and 'we'
* descriptive touches
* clever use of individual words and phrases.

These are the final touches to a thorough analysis of the texts.

Remember that to fulfil the demands of the third question you will have to make sure that you cross-reference the specified aspect of the material comparing and contrasting the strategies used by both writers.

Analysing media and non-fiction texts

2 Consider the use made of fact and opinion

Now, think about the actual content.
Consider the use made of:
* statistics
* the findings of 'experts'
* personal recommendation
* claims
* sweeping statements
* the forceful expression of opinion as fact
* the use of interviews and eye-witness accounts.

Remember that writers will use both fact and opinion in their development of a point of view. How effective have they been in achieving their desired outcome? Are you convinced or persuaded? What are the telling points and why? If it is an argument, is it presented convincingly or rather weakly – just an appeal to our fears or emotions?

3 Look out for the use made of presentational, structural and linguistic devices

Consider the use made of:
* headlines, headings and subheadings
* pictures and colour
* lists and bullet points
* bold and italic text
* font styles
* varying sentence length
* unusual punctuation
* simile and metaphor
* adjectives and adverbs
* puns and word play
* rhetorical questions
* contrast
* exaggeration
* repetition
* dramatic openings and endings.

These will have been used to enhance the effectiveness of the writing. Spotting their use will reinforce the depth of your understanding of the writer's purpose.

6 Comparing paired passages

In Paper 2 Section B of the exam, you will have to analyse and comment on two texts as well as making a comparison between them. These texts will usually be based on the same subject but are likely to take very different approaches and will feature different forms of writing.

As well as analysing features from each text, you are required to compare and contrast an aspect or aspects of the two texts. You could do this by first discussing each text separately and then drawing comparisons between them, but perhaps a more effective approach is to discuss them together.

In the example that follows, suggestions are given as to how you might set about comparing the given texts, Text A and Text B, and making cross-references between them.

Text A – An advertisement for a new airline company

Flights of fantasy with Comfi-Jet

Tired of being squashed like sardines on bargain-basement flights? Fed up with mile-long queues at check-in desks? Had enough of plastic trays of tasteless 'food' dished out by uninterested cabin staff on the so-called major airlines? Fed up with paying ridiculous prices for delays and discomforts?

If so, then look no further than the newest, most exciting airline on the scene, Comfi-Jet, where YOU, the deserving customer, can travel in the comfort and style that you have always dreamed of – and at a price that will put our rivals to shame.

Launched just six months ago, Comfi-Jet is now really taking off, and already thousands of satisfied travellers are singing the praises of our services. 'First time I've actually enjoyed flying,' says Mr Salcombe of Birmingham, while Mrs Dillon of Belfast claims, 'Our flight to Malaga with Comfi-Jet was almost as good as the holiday!' Proof of our progress is the fascinating statistic that the number of passengers travelling with Comfi-Jet has <u>doubled each month</u> since we commenced operations. We are indeed soaring above our rivals.

We fly to 26 destinations in no less than 10 countries throughout Europe and have plans to commence regular flights to the USA and Canada next year. Belfast is particularly well served, with daily flights to London Gatwick (for as little as £40 return!) and twice weekly flights to Paris and Amsterdam, all from the convenient departure point of the City Airport.

Whether you're a business executive city-hopping to important conferences or a couple of newly-weds jetting off on a romantic honeymoon, Comfi-Jet is the airline for you. We operate a substantial fleet of sleek, modern aircraft, all featuring state-of-the-art internal design, ensuring that all passengers have plenty of leg-room and can enjoy the comfort of the spacious cabin.

On board, relax and enjoy the sheer luxury of the first-class service provided by our specially trained cabin attendants. Unlike the many 'low-cost, no-frills, budget airlines' in existence at the moment, where you simply starve until the end of your journey, on a Comfi-Jet trip you will be pampered throughout your flight. Not only do we provide freshly prepared food, but also it is our proud boast that we are one of the few airlines to actually offer a menu on all flights, so that you, the customer, can decide exactly what delicacy to choose from our extensive range.

Above all, Comfi-Jet try to take the hassle and stress out of flying, so that passengers can access their flights without the ritual of queuing. Once you have booked your flight on the Internet, all you have to do is arrive at the airport a few minutes before departure time and go directly to your plane, where the latest onboard technology will check you in. In fact, you just show and go! Nothing could be easier!

So, next time you fly, choose Comfi-Jet. Check us out now on our popular website www.comfijet.com

Text B – A letter of complaint from a dissatisfied Comfi-Jet passenger

The Managing Director

Comfi-Jet Flights

Belfast City Airport

Sir,

I recently had the misfortune to travel on your airline, Comfi-Jet, on flight JA 223 from Belfast City to Amsterdam, on Tuesday 5th August. My flight was an absolute nightmare and I wish to protest most strongly about the way my fellow passengers and I were treated by your company.

My nightmare began when I arrived at Belfast City Airport, only to be told that, due to 'scheduling changes', the plane was leaving from the International Airport at Aldergrove. My unfortunate fellow passengers and I had to be bussed there, where we had to wait another hour before our aircraft was ready for boarding.

I was even more outraged to discover that our plane was certainly not a 'sleek, modern' jet (instead it was a lumbering, propeller-driven antique) and it was anything but 'Comfi'!

When we were eventually allowed on board we found the aircraft in a disgustingly filthy state. It obviously had not been cleaned after the last flight. When I complained about this to a gum-chewing cabin steward his response was a grunt and a shrug of his shoulders. I suggest that a course in basic manners should be a top priority for your staff.

I was puzzled at the start that the plane was less than half full. This mystery was explained about 40 minutes into the flight, when the pilot announced that we would be calling at Glasgow airport to pick up other passengers. This was supposed to be a 'direct' and 'convenient' flight, but this diversion added another hour to our already intolerable journey. How dare you subject passengers to such misery, just so that your flights make a profit! I shall certainly be reporting your company to the Advertising Standards Authority for the totally misleading information given in your brochure.

By the time we had left Glasgow, I was feeling hungry but my hunger pangs disappeared after a quick glance at the plastic tray thrust at me by a surly stewardess. For a moment I considered eating the plastic knife, fork and spoon, on the grounds that they would be considerably more nutritious, and certainly less harmful to my digestive system, than the unidentifiable sludge offered to me as food.

I was also extremely disappointed that there was no special help offered on your supposedly 'caring' airline for disabled people like myself – I just had to endure the narrow, cramped and uncomfortable seats.

I eventually arrived in Amsterdam four hours late, stressed out and utterly exhausted. Once there, I immediately booked a return flight with a decent airline! I shall never fly Comfi-Jet again. Your allegedly 'exciting' airline is in fact a total disgrace – the worst I've come across in thirty years of flying!

I expect to hear from you soon with an offer of compensation for all the inconvenience I suffered. If not, my solicitor will be taking up the matter!

Yours,

Joanne Wright (Mrs)

Some useful cross-references

▶ **Purpose/intention of each writer:** Text A is advertising material and the writer is trying to persuade the reader to fly with Comfi-Jet. The writer of Text B has a more personal purpose, to complain about her flight and to demand compensation.

▶ **Target audience:** Text A is aimed at a very wide audience, the general public. Text B is directed specifically towards one person and the airline company he represents.

▶ **Tone:** The tone of Text A is friendly and appealing, making the potential passenger feel really special – note the phrase '*YOU, the deserving customer*'. The tone of Text B is angry and aggressive – note the phrase '*How dare you... !*'

▶ **Totally opposing attitudes:** The writer of Text A says that flying with Comfi-Jet is a '*fantasy*', something passengers '*have always dreamed of*', while the writer of Text B claims her experience was a '*nightmare*'.

▶ **Facts and opinions:** Although Text A is largely opinion, the writer does give some precise facts about the airline – '*26 destinations in no less than 10 countries*' for prices that start at '*£40 return*' and the statistic that the number of passengers has doubled each month. The writer of Text B also gives some facts, for example the diversion via Glasgow, but much of what she has to say is personal opinion – for example the description of the airline food as '*unidentifiable sludge*'.

▶ **Range of opinions:** The writer of Text A uses a well-known advertising technique, introducing the opinions of some selected satisfied customers who *sing the praises* of the company. The writer of Text B presents only her own strong opinions in her attack on the company.

▶ **Touches of humour:** In Text A there are several puns that help to make the writing more lively and light-hearted – '*really taking off*' and '*soaring above our rivals*'. However, any humour in Text B is viciously sarcastic in its tone – the suggestion that the plastic cutlery would have been more '*nutritious, and certainly less harmful to my digestive system*' than the actual food.

▶ **Major areas of disagreement:** The writers have opposing views about:
  ● the planes – '*sleek, modern aircraft*'/'*lumbering, propeller-driven antique*'
  ● comfort – '*the comfort of the spacious cabin*'/'*cramped and uncomfortable seats*'
  ● the cabin staff – '*specially trained cabin attendants*'/'*surly stewardess*'
  ● the food – '*what delicacy to choose*'/'*unidentifiable sludge*'
  ● convenience – '*Belfast is particularly well served*', '*In fact, you just show and go!*'/'*scheduling changes*', '*this diversion*'.

▶ **Language contrasts:**
  ● The writer of Text A suggests that it will be a privilege for passengers to travel in '*comfort and style*' with Comfi-Jet, but the lady in Text B has a very different opinion – it was a '*misfortune*' to travel with Comfi-Jet.
  ● Text A uses leading questions at the beginning to convince the reader that the major airlines do not match Comfi-Jet's service – '*Fed-up with mile-long queues at check-in desks?*' In Text B however, angry exclamations are a common feature of the writing – '*If not, my solicitor will be taking up the matter!*'
  ● Text A features lavish promises – '*enjoy the sheer luxury of the first-class service*', whereas Text B features threats – '*I shall certainly be reporting your company*'.
  ● The writer of Text A criticises other airlines for poor service – '*tasteless "food" dished out*

by disinterested cabin staff – but the writer of Text B accuses Comfi-Jet of similar faults – *'the plastic tray thrust at me by a surly stewardess'*.

● The tone of confidence in Text A – *'it is our proud boast'* – contrasts with the scathingly dismissive attitude in Text B – *'your…airline is…a total disgrace!'*

● In Text A Comfi-Jet claim that they *'take the hassle and stress out of flying'*, but the writer of Text B strongly disagrees, saying she arrived at her destination *'stressed out and utterly exhausted'*.

● Flattering descriptive terms are used in Text A – *'state-of-the-art'*, *'freshly prepared'*, *'spacious'* – as compared with bluntly critical descriptions in Text B – *'disgustingly filthy'*, *'intolerable'*, *'totally misleading'*.

● The writer of Text A makes use of superlatives (words suggesting that Comfi-Jet is the best) – *'newest, most exciting'* – but Mrs Wright in Text B claims that Comfi-Jet is *'the worst I've come across'*.

● Text A tries to make flying seem exciting or romantic – *'city-hopping to important conferences'* or *'jetting off on a romantic honeymoon'*. But Mrs Wright describes her flight as miserable – *'an intolerable journey'*.

● There is much use of alliteration and other language devices in Text A, to make the writing pleasant and catchy – *'squashed like sardines'*, *'Proof of our progress'*, and especially *'just show and go!'* The writing in Text B is much more blunt and does not use such consciously decorative language.

▸ **Conclusions:** Text A finishes in a friendly, inviting, confident style – *'choose Comfi-Jet. Check us out now'*. But Text B ends with a sting in the tail – the threat of legal action if *'an offer of compensation'* is not forthcoming.

ACTIVITY 8

Now, you can try some cross-referencing. These two texts present very different views of Comfi-Jet. Compare the nature of the evidence used in both texts. How convinced are you by the evidence presented? Remember to select examples of these contrasts and to make appropriate comments on them.

Answering effectively

a   Write a short purposeful opening paragraph. Below are two very different introductions.

✗   *In this piece of writing I am going to consider the evidence put forward in Text A and then I will examine the evidence put forward in Text B.*

✓   *The writer of Text A firmly believes that we should all be doing aerobics, whilst the writer of Text B thinks that this form of exercise is little more than the latest trendy fashion in designer fitness. She believes we would all be better off taking a brisk walk three times a week.*

The first of these introductions shows no understanding and therefore is not going to attract any marks. By contrast, the second opening paragraph demonstrates that the student understands the writers' stances and the major differences in the texts.

b   It is not enough to make analytical comments and leave them unsupported. Equally it is unsatisfactory to quote words and phrases without adequate supporting comment. Below are some examples of how to, and how not to, go about this. (The students are attempting to comment on a newspaper report about a tragedy.)

✗ *The writer uses strong words that make her feelings about the tragedy clear.*

✗ *Words and phrases like 'ill-advised', 'foolish' and 'rash and unnecessary' are good words.*

In these two comments the students are attempting to describe the writer's stance but their general nature means that they are not sufficiently developed to explain exactly what is meant. They could be successfully combined as follows:

✓ *Words and phrases like 'ill-advised', 'foolish' and 'rash and unnecessary' make it clear that the writer is strongly condemning those in charge. She clearly feels that they have to accept responsibility for this tragedy.*

c The use of embedded quotations is a quick and effective way of getting a point across. The following example is analysing a review of a book.

✓ *The writer of Text A uses a series of very positive adjectives to describe the book: 'amazing', 'dramatic' and 'non-stop'. She reinforces this favourable impression when she states that she 'was deeply affected' by the work and thought it much more than 'a standard thriller'.*

d When presenting evidence to back up an answer, keep your quotations to the minimum. Below you will find two further examples. Both are commenting on the opening remarks made in a book review.

✗ *We know the writer of Text B does not like the book when he says, 'By the time I had read the first two pages my attention was beginning to wander: I was bored by the time I had waded my weary way to the end of the first chapter, and by the twentieth page I was beginning to lose the will to live!'*

✓ *The writer of Text B immediately makes his complete dislike obvious with his blunt, exaggerated and scornful opening sentence.*

The first comment could be credited for showing a straightforward understanding of the writer's viewpoint. The second comment, in half the space, tells the reader twice as much. This student has commented on the writer's stance as well as analysing the style and tone adopted by the writer.

e There will be two texts to consider and it is essential that you make comparisons between them. This is done by cross-referencing material from the texts.

✓ *Both writers try to strengthen their viewpoint by referring to comments made by other critics who share their opinions. We are meant to be convinced by the 'well-known Peter Ellis' in Text A and 'that famous thriller writer, Michael Page' in Text B.*

✓ *The writer of Text A is enthusiastic in her description of the thriller's plot, describing it as 'full of tension' and 'genuinely original' whereas the writer of Text B refers to it as 'far-fetched', 'uninspired' and 'frankly disappointing'.*

✓ *The only point that the writers of these texts do agree on is that they both enjoy the appearances of the retired teacher, the forgetful Mrs Dorking. She provides the thriller with 'moments of comic genius' according to the excited writer of Text A or 'all too rare flashes of comic relief' as the writer of Text B less generously describes her contribution.*

These three comments demonstrate how to effectively draw together points of comparison or contrast across texts.

7 Time to get practical

In the fourth section of this book, you have learnt the skills required in answering the type of questions that appear in Paper 2 Section B. It is important that you practise these skills on complete texts and preferably under examination conditions. In the actual examination, you will only have **one hour** for this section of the paper.

Below is a series of key points to use as a revision checklist.

▸ You can expect to find **two different forms of text**, which will both be about the same topic. Very often, but not always, they will put forward very different views on that topic. Your task is to assess the techniques and methods used by the writers.

▸ You will be required to answer three questions. The first two questions will focus on each of the texts in turn, and the third will require a comparison of an element from both texts.

▸ The examiner does **not** want your opinion on the topic. The texts may well deal with a subject that you have strong views about: don't include them because they are not relevant and you will not be credited for this type of personal comment.

▸ Your job is to **analyse** how the writers have developed their texts.

▸ **Identify** the standpoint that the writer has taken in each case.

▸ **Review** the texts and think about **how** each of the writers has attempted to convince you that what they are putting forward is well founded.

▸ **Identify** the different strategies that have been used. In the exam, feel free to highlight points, phrases and words that are significant to each writer's purpose.

▸ Do **not** make the mistake of reporting the contents of each text.

▸ **Cross-reference** and **select** the examples from each text that you plan to use to illustrate your conclusions.

▸ **Compare** the two texts. This can be done either:
  ● by working through each text in turn, making sure you point out contrasts and/or comparisons with the first text that you assessed; or
  ● by selecting points common to both texts and analysing the different approaches and methods adopted by the writers in their attempt to develop a point of view on these issues.

The two test pieces that follow are typical of Paper 2 Section B.

FOUNDATION TIER SAMPLE PAPER

Paper 2   Section B

This section tests reading skills.

- Spend about **15 minutes** studying both texts carefully.

- Answer **all three** questions.

---

1   Answer using **Text A**. Spend **15 minutes** on your answer. Text A is a brochure
    promoting holidays in country cottages.

    How does Text A try to persuade the reader to take a holiday in this company's
    country cottages?

    In your answer consider:

    - the use of colour and layout (including the headline)

    - the use made of fact and opinion.

                                                                      [10 marks]

2   Answer using **Text B**. Spend **15 minutes** on your answer. Text B is a diary excerpt
    that describes a family's experience of this type of accommodation.

    Text B describes a disastrous holiday experience. How does the writer hold the
    reader's attention?

    In your answer consider:

    - the way the writer uses structure

    - the type of evidence that the writer uses to develop his viewpoint.

                                                                      [10 marks]

3   Answer using **Text A** and **Text B**. Spend **15 minutes** on your answer.

    These texts have presented very different views on this type of holiday. Compare
    how the writers have used words and phrases in order to strengthen their
    different viewpoints?

                                                                      [10 marks]

Text A – An extract from a holiday brochure

Finding a holiday home-from-home!

Look no further than '<u>Country Cottages Unlimited</u>'

Do YOU want to get away from it all? Do you fancy a relaxing dream holiday in the heart of the countryside? Do you want a simple, hassle-free weekend break, arranged for you by caring people with years of experience?

Then all you need to do is make one simple freephone call to our expert sales assistants at Country Cottages Unlimited. They will help you select a holiday cottage that meets your requirements and your budget. We have been running an increasingly successful business since 1960 and we pride ourselves on matching your individual tastes to the ideal holiday destination, a fact confirmed by the thousands of satisfied customers who have written to us.

We offer a huge variety of fascinating locations for your holiday. Whatever you want – the beauty of rolling green meadows, the wild and lonely sweep of moorlands or the savage spectacle of mountain range and coastline – it is only a phone call away.

Our cottages are available all year round and the choice we offer is truly outstanding. Gathered together in the pages of our brochure is a fine collection of holiday properties spanning the length and breadth of our beautiful islands. Even if

you can only be away for a few days, think of how satisfying we can make that welcome break from routine. Strolling through thick carpets of spring bluebells in an ancient English woodland, enjoying a heart-warming winter evening's craic in an Irish village pub, exploring the mystic, hidden places of the Scottish Highlands or sampling the myths and legends of the ancient kingdom of Wales – these are all on offer in our latest exciting brochure.

Our cottages are all comfortably furnished, cosy and welcoming at any time of year, and each has its own special character and setting. Most feature all the mod cons required to make your stay as relaxing as possible: dishwashers, automatic washing machines, televisions, sound systems, even jacuzzis. All you have to do is put your feet up and eventually come home with your spirits refreshed and restored.

Our bigger-than-ever 2004/5 brochure offers more than 3000 fully equipped and spotlessly clean cottages, with prices starting from an amazing £150 per week. And we know that size matters to our customers! So whether it is to be a secluded romantic hideaway for two or a spacious converted mill, complete with swimming pool and fitness suite, for a party of ten, you will find it in our tastefully presented catalogue.

We cater for every need and taste. A single-storey cottage with easy access for the disabled, a large garden for those lively summer barbecues, a tennis court to keep the kids occupied, or just a secluded situation with a stunning view – all can be found in our extensive list.

For even more convenience, there's a website to use in conjunction with this brochure. For each cottage there will be more information and in many cases a 'virtual tour', so that you can look around your dream destination before you actually go there! You can also find details of local facilities, such as restaurants, leisure centres, shops and attractions.

We understand that you expect only the best and that's the service we strive to offer. Contact us by telephone today on 0888 1211 3344 or click on <u>www.country cottages-unlimited.co.uk</u>. We're waiting to help you!

Text B – This is a diary entry

Monday, 24th July 2000: A short break in Devon

I should have known better than to have been looking forward to our family week away in a quaint cottage in the country. Long, leisurely days, I thought. Relaxing strolls down peaceful, pinewood pathways with the children, I thought. The healthy countryside air, I thought. That's what the brochure had confidently promised, surely not too much to expect – wrong! You'd think a forty-something year old would be too wily to be suckered by silky words and glossy pictures – wrong again!

Rose Cottage – it sounded wonderful, but to be honest, Not-So-Rosy Cottage would have been more appropriate! It was miles from anywhere, in the middle of a desolate bog! Already, it had taken us half a day to find it and at that moment I wished we hadn't! It was instantly clear that the only 'activity' available locally was walking (through a bog, in the rain!) and the only escape was a twenty-five mile drive on appalling roads to the nearest town.

Things had not got off to the most promising of starts, I can remember thinking. I was right and worse was to come. The 'secluded hideaway' was skulking, sodden, at the end of an over-grown lane. The torrential rain was falling as enthusiastically as ever as I strode manfully forward exuding a ridiculously positive approach to the place. Looking back on it, I'm not really surprised that this led to some sarcastic comments from the cynical offspring and a wry smirk from my long-suffering partner.

As soon as I pushed the door open I knew my efforts were utterly useless. I was instantly transported back to some of those ghastly slums that had passed for student flats in my earlier years. The place was cold, dark and dingy. I gingerly entered. The smell of rather stale smoke and beer only reinforced my initial, negative impression. In the cheerless living room, even the carpets and furnishings were scruffy and worn. A check of the kitchen was no more encouraging and my children came down the creaking stairs complaining of a 'grotty' bathroom and damp bedrooms and bed linen. I cringed; remembering that this week's dose of 'old-world charm' had cost the better part of £500!

I can deal with sad, puppy-dog eyes from one section of the family, but not from the entire group. Moments like these are defining. I knew something drastic was called for! My credibility was on the line. I did what I had to do! I ushered the family out, locked the door of the hovel that was Rose Cottage and fled back to civilisation!

The traffic was mercifully light. As a result, by 9.30pm, we were eating tasty fish and chips – perfectly at home!

HIGHER TIER SAMPLE PAPER

Paper 2   Section B

This section tests **reading** skills.

- Spend about **15 minutes** studying both texts carefully.

- Answer **all three** questions.

_____

1   Answer using **Text A**. Spend **15 minutes** on your answer. Text A is an advertising leaflet.

   Text A encourages its readers to adopt a more active lifestyle. In your answer write about:

   - the particular audience at which it is aimed

   - the use of colour, illustration and layout to promote the message.

   [10 marks]

2   Answer using **Text B**. Spend **15 minutes** on your answer. Text B is a piece of autobiographical writing.

   Text B presents a personal view on the merits of exercise. How does the writer engage our interest and develop her point of view?

   In your answer consider:

   - the use made of fact and opinion

   - the use of words and phrases.

   [10 marks]

3   Answer using **Text A and Text B**. Spend about **15 minutes** on your answer.

   The texts come to very different conclusions about the issue of exercise. Compare the types of evidence that are presented and say which you find more convincing and why.

   [10 marks]

Text A – *The front cover and two double pages from a brochure promoting the idea of well-being through fitness*

think AGAIN!

There are many reasons why people find it hard to be as physically active as they'd like to be. These are some you're likely to hear, together with the comments we'd like to make.

"I'm too tired when I come home from work."
You may be surprised to find that being more active actually gives you more energy. Try walking or cycling to work and see if you still feel as tired.

"I don't have the time."
You don't have to spend hours in the gym. Building activity into your life, by walking or cycling to get around, can reap rewards.

"I'm too old."
You're never too old to feel the benefits of healthy activity. Take up a new activity, but start gently.

"I do enough exercise already."
Most people overestimate the amount of physical activity that they do, and could benefit from doing more. Take a look at an average week. How often can you say that you do enough activity that leaves you feeling warm and slightly out of breath?

"Once you start to become more active you'll soon feel the benefits, and you'll be surprised just how much you are enjoying yourself!"

Remember

- **You don't have to be fit to start with**
  The most important thing is to build up your level of activity gradually. You'll soon notice the difference in how you feel.

- **You don't have to leave home to exercise**
  There are plenty of activities inside and outside the house that could be an opportunity for exercise, and if you involve your children in your exercise routine, it can be great fun.

- **You don't need to set aside a lot of time for exercise**
  Activities can quite easily be introduced into your daily routine, even if you are working. Walking, cycling and jogging can be an alternative to taking the car; a quick trip to the pool at lunch time or after work can be a good way to exercise and unwind.

- **You don't have to be young**
  It's never too late to take up a new activity. Older people can benefit greatly from physical activity, and often have the time and freedom to pursue a range of interests.

family LIFE

When you have children to look after, it can seem as though you have very little energy left for exercise, and even less time!

But exercise can help you to relax, as well as providing you with energy for the rest of the day. It could be an activity for you and the children to share at home, or you could take part in a class or exercise with friends.

If you adapt the activity to fit your lifestyle, then spending 30 minutes of your day being active can become an enjoyable part of your routine.

- Pram pushing could have been designed with exercise in mind - just as long as you make it a brisk push rather than a stroll.

- Most leisure centres have a creche where children can play safely while you take part in an exercise class, have a swim, or take part in a sport you enjoy.

- Once your children start going to a playgroup, you'll have a few hours to yourself. Why not use this time to exercise - it can be a great way to charge your batteries.

Be Safe!

You will be able to enjoy your activities safely if you follow a few commonsense guidelines:

- If you have a virus or feel unwell, do not force yourself to be active. Take time off to get better.
- Never exercise if you have been drinking alcohol or if you have just eaten a heavy meal.
- Drink plenty of fluids - aim to drink between six and eight glasses of water a day.
- If walking or jogging in the dark, make sure you can be seen and that you avoid busy or dangerous roads. Try to find someone to accompany you.

Text B – *This excerpt is a piece of autobiographical writing*

An RAF fitness instructor I once met had a name for civilians who take little or no exercise. He rather scathingly described them as Fat Jobbers. Well, I am Enemy Number One, for I take no exercise whatsoever. I'm not a slob – I watch little television and never eat pizzas in front of it when I do – but I am still the ultimate Fat Jobber. If I can help it I barely move at all, and certainly never in the sustained sort of way which requires special shoes. I am just one of those people, and there are plenty of us, unfashionable types though we be, who are not primed for physical exertion. I hate sport and always have done. I don't drink, eat breakfast, smoke, take drugs. I'm damned if I'm going to miss out on all that fun and take exercise as well.

I think it's important that fitness fanatics know what it's like for those who find exercise repulsive. My hope is that they might stop bugging the Fat Jobbers with pious assertions about how much better we would feel were we to go to the gym.

When I was at school, we were forced out into the freezing cold with daft short skirts, stiff fingers and empurpled knees to play netball, hockey or ludicrous lacrosse. It's not the winning, it's the taking part, we were told. I didn't give a fig for either. At least when doing Latin translations, tedious in their own way, you could be sitting down on a soft sofa. By a radiator. You were warm. That's when I felt 'better'.

But even summer sports never appealed. Tennis was OK, but only to watch, preferably while eating strawberries. As for swimming, I remain a deep snob about public swimming pools, squeamish about revealing my imperfect body in one of life's dread items of clothing, the bathing suit; about the fuss of dressing, undressing, wrestling with clammy towels; about the noise; the enduring stench of chlorine; but mostly about the feeling of swishing around in one enormous urinal. I don't do swimming.

Since leaving school, I have tried exercising just twice. I joined a hugely expensive gym and went at seven every morning, 'using' it in the same unhealthy way as addicts use illicit substances. I really hate gyms. They are cynical vanity factories. They hook people in with promises of leaner bodies, and take large membership fees knowing that most sane people can't sustain the level of boredom required for pumping iron for more than few weeks.

I lasted six weeks and felt poorer at the end of it. When the next delusions of exercise came upon me a few years later, I opted for an altogether cheaper version; running. People told me that in two weeks I would feel like a different person. For the first five months I was gagging for breath with every step, but carried on doggedly. By the sixth month, the forty-five minutes became less agonizing sometimes, but not always. I did it for a year and reaped no benefits. My body did not change, except for my knee joints, which complained bitterly. On only two occasions was I even aware that I was fit. I went on a skiing holiday and found I could easily walk up a mountain. Useful. And on a rare walk in France one summer, I strode up a steep hill leaving my friends trailing behind. That felt good. But a whole year of running only for those two brief moments of satisfaction?

It just didn't compute . . .

That was ten years ago. Since then, I have had three children, so I 'do steps' several times a day just walking up and down the stairs, and I do a lot of 'weight lifting' (several stones' worth of four-year-old, two-year-old and five-month-old) without really noticing.

Perhaps in this age of obesity, it's irresponsible of me to back the inactive life, but I find exercise tedious and unrewarding. I'm not fit and I'm quite fat – a fat jobber even – but though I don't go in for pavement pounding and other exertions, I'm not a complete slob. I just find execise for exercise's sake appalling, and remain one of those people who feels a lot 'better' when I'm not consciously putting myself through it. The whole fitness thing is a mystery to me, and long may it remain so.

From 'Can't Jog, Won't Jog?' by Candida Crewe in *The Times Magazine*, 19 October 2002